Collins

I0800199

The Core in Practice

Educator's Guide to Personal and Professional Skills

Gary Halcrow, Stewart Paterson, Wilma Shen and Becky Youngman

For the IB Career-related Programme

William Collins' dream of knowledge for all began with the publication of his first book in 1819. A self-educated mill worker, he not only enriched millions of lives, but also founded a flourishing publishing house. Today, staying true to this spirit, Collins books are packed with inspiration, innovation and practical expertise. They place you at the centre of a world of possibility and give you exactly what you need to explore it.

Published by Collins
An imprint of HarperCollins*Publishers*
The News Building, 1 London Bridge Street, London, SE1 9GF, UK

HarperCollins*Publishers*
Macken House, 39/40 Mayor Street Upper, Dublin 1, D01 C9W8, Ireland

Browse the complete Collins catalogue at
collins.co.uk

10 9 8 7 6 5 4 3 2 1

A catalogue record for this publication is available from the British Library.

ISBN 978-0-00-877028-0

Authors: Gary Halcrow, Stewart Paterson, Wilma Shen and Becky Youngman

Publisher: Catherine Martin

Senior Product Developer: Daniela Mora Chavarría

Development editor: Sonya Newland

Copyeditor: Mark Gadd

Proofreader: Catherine Dakin

Cover designer: Amparo Barreras (Kneath Associates)

Typesetter and illustrator: Six Red Marbles

Production controller: Alhady Ali

Printed and bound in the UK by Ashford Colour Ltd

Acknowledgements

With thanks to Donald Blackmon for their review comments.

The publishers gratefully acknowledge the permission granted to reproduce the copyright material in this book. Every effort has been made to trace copyright holders and to obtain their permission for the use of copyright material. The publishers will gladly receive any information enabling them to rectify any error or omission at the first opportunity.

We are grateful to the International Baccalaureate Organization for their permission to reproduce copyright material under licence, including the Aims of the Reflective Project, the IB Learner Profile, the Approaches to Learning (ATL) skills, the Structure and stages of the Reflective Project, the Relationship of the Reflective Project to the four elements of the Career-related Programme, the Career-related Programme model graphic, the Reflective Project assessment criteria and markbands, guidance on achievement in the Reflective Project, the definition of reflection and reflexivity, the Personal and Professional Skills (PPS) course requirements, the PPS learning outcomes, and the stages of structuring inquiries from the IB Reflective Project Guide and the Personal and Professional Skills (PPS) Guide © International Baccalaureate Organization, 2025.

MIX
Paper | Supporting responsible forestry
FSC www.fsc.org
FSC® C011748

Contents

How to use this resource

This resource mainly focuses on the personal and professional skills (PPS) and reflective project (RP) components of the Career-related Programme (CP) core, although it also highlights relevant links with language and cultural studies (LCS) and community engagement (CE).

The PPS course is the main intersection of the CP core, through which learning can be connected and explored across all contexts. The RP is a culminating experience, pulling together the knowledge, understanding and experience gained from all areas of the CP. These factors combine to make PPS and the RP the perfect vehicles through which to explore the CP core components and the broader implementation of the CP programme.

Here you will find information, examples, suggestions, prompt questions, templates and tips to help you establish effective practice when implementing the PPS course, the RP and the CP core. To get the most from this resource, it is important to read the IB guides and supporting documents for these components to ensure you understand the latest guidance and have access to any necessary supporting documents.

It may also be useful to consider the following questions before you begin, as well as while working through the information in the subsequent chapters.

- Do you know the 'why' behind the decision to introduce the CP at your school?
- Could you write a student profile for the ideal CP candidate within your school context?
- Is your school's vision for the CP shared by the entire school community?
- What would the successful implementation of the PPS and RP components look like in your school?
- Can you identify the key stakeholders who will support you in achieving your vision for PPS, the RP and the wider implementation of the CP at your school?

Meet the authors

This resource is the work of four experienced and passionate IB educators who have held various roles within IB schools. All four share a love of the CP and what it can bring to a school community, and are delighted to be able to support IB schools in implementing this programme.

Stewart Paterson

Stewart is an experienced IBDP/CP coordinator with nearly a decade of expertise in implementing the International Baccalaureate Career-related Programme (IBCP) across schools in the Asia-Pacific region. Stewart is the chair of the IBDP regional network in East China and has obtained the National Professional Qualification for Headship (NPQH).

Stewart is deeply passionate about the transformative potential of personalised, career-focused pathways in post-16 education. He believes the CP framework offers a powerful model for schools to design academically rigorous and relevant programmes in collaboration with university and industry partners. Stewart has consulted multiple universities on their entry into the IBCP market as Career-related Studies providers and hopes to support many more in the coming years.

Wilma Shen

Wilma has dedicated over 25 years to the field of education, working in various roles including administration, counselling, teaching and leadership. Her journey with the IBCP began 13 years ago, when her school became the first flagship institution in Hong Kong and East Asia to offer the CP. Witnessing first-hand how her students thrive and benefit from this innovative and highly customisable programme, Wilma quickly became a passionate advocate for the CP's transformative potential.

Wilma has taken on leadership roles, including chair of the 7-CP School Alliance in Hong Kong and co-chair of the IB CP Schools Network in the Asia-Pacific region.

She welcomes opportunities to help schools grow and strengthen their CP offerings. Wilma firmly believes that educators have a responsibility to provide students with meaningful opportunities to apply their learning beyond the classroom, empowering them to become agile, resourceful individuals ready to thrive in an ever-changing world.

Gary Halcrow

Gary is an experienced CP coordinator with over 12 years of teaching and leadership experience in international education. Growing up as the son of two Physical Education teachers, Gary discovered his passion for teaching at 16, which led him to graduate from the University of Edinburgh's School of Education. While his early career was rooted in teaching Physical Education, Gary's current focus lies in coordinating the CP, with a particular emphasis on teaching PPS, developing multiple PPS curricula tailored to student needs and interests, and leading students and supervisors through the RP process.

As a dedicated CP coordinator, Gary is passionate about the CP core, believing that PPS and the RP serve as the cornerstone of meaningful, student-centred learning. His leadership includes guiding secondary teams through successful IB evaluation visits and fostering a school environment that caters to the best interests of all students, removing barriers to learning, and ensuring every student has opportunities to succeed through meaningful and relevant education.

Becky Youngman

Dr Becky Youngman has four decades of experience in education. She taught in the Middle Years Programme and Diploma Programme for 21 years before becoming the curriculum manager for accelerated academics and college and career readiness programmes in a large urban school district in the United States.

Dr Youngman then held a curriculum manager position for the CP. She was responsible for developing the 2025 PPS and RP components and the corresponding support materials and professional development resources.

She champions the CP as an opportunity for all students to participate in a rigorous and engaging education that meets their interests and needs. She believes that the strength of the CP lies in its holistic nature and its ability to empower students in creating their own future pathways.

1 Introduction to the International Baccalaureate Career-related Programme

This chapter covers the following:

- The purpose of the IB Career-related Programme
- Comparing the Diploma Programme and the Career-related Programme
- Personal and professional skills and the reflective project

This chapter is intended for all staff involved in the implementation of the Career-related Programme.

The purpose of the IB Career-related Programme

The IB Career-related Programme (CP) is a **framework** to help schools meet the needs of all students aged 16 to 19. It is the perfect academic programme for students with a specialist interest in a career field. The CP is academic and personalised in nature, allowing students to learn more within the context of what truly matters to them, setting them up for success in their further studies and future careers. The CP framework allows schools to personalise academic and career programmes and learning pathways for their students. It has the potential to have a transformational impact on any school community.

What is the Career-related Programme?

The CP is a three-part educational framework consisting of the Career-related Study (CRS), a minimum of two International Baccalaureate Diploma Programme (DP) courses and the CP core, which is made of four components:

- personal and professional skills (PPS)
- reflective project (RP)
- language and cultural studies (LCS)
- community engagement (CE).

The Career-related Programme model

The Career-related Study (CRS) is a unique feature of the CP. It allows schools to partner with universities, professional and government bodies, and other awarding exam boards to provide specialised and often fast-tracked routes into a variety of career fields. The purpose of the CRS course is to immerse students in academic and professional learning directly related to their chosen career field and area of interest.

Some CRS focus on a specific career field, while others focus on a particular skillset that can be applied across many fields, such as data analysis and interpretation, digital communications, coding, cybersecurity, user experience (UX) and artificial intelligence engineering. These CRS pathways allow students to benefit from the depth of learning available in the CP while maintaining some breadth in their future study and career options.

The CRS can also be delivered in a variety of modes. Some CRS pathways are taught on campus by an educator from the school and certified by an awarding body, while others are taught on campus directly by staff from the CRS provider. Additionally, some CRS pathways are available online (synchronous, asynchronous or a combination of both), and a few offer a hybrid delivery option that combines online and on-campus study. The way in which your students access their CRS will depend on your chosen strategic partners, geographical location, staffing and available resources.

Each school will choose the most appropriate CRS for their context to make the CP as impactful as possible for their school community. Some schools offer one or two career pathways, whereas others encompass more than 20. These decisions will depend on your students' needs, interests and aspirations, as well as the context of their school.

For any school in candidacy for authorisation, it is also advisable to speak with an IB consultant and IB World Schools manager to make a good decision about what works best for their school's context.

How is the Career-related Programme implemented?

CP students will study two, three or four DP courses alongside their chosen CRS. Students have flexibility when choosing between **Standard Level (SL)** and **Higher Level (HL)** DP courses, so you could see a CP student with two SL courses or four HL ones. Any decision on the number or level of DP courses will be affected by the number of hours students will dedicate to their chosen CRS and their aspirations for further study. Ideally, the DP courses taken in the context of the CP support students in developing the knowledge and understanding required to complement their CRS and prepare them for secondary completion, further study and their future career field.

All CP students will complete the four compulsory core components: PPS, RP, LCS and CE.

The CP core is **holistic** in nature, with each component having its own unique purpose. The core is combined with the CRS and DP courses to ensure that the framework is an academic, holistic, personalised and rich programme of learning for any student. The CP is designed to ensure that students graduate with the academic rigour required for further study, the professional skills and expertise necessary for success within their chosen career fields, and skills that will enable them to achieve continued growth and fulfilment in their personal lives.

Comparing the Diploma Programme and the Career-related Programme

A common misconception among IB schools offering – or considering offering – these two programmes is that the CP is a less academic version of the DP. This could not be further from the truth. The DP is academic and broad, while the CP is academic and specialised. The DP supports students who are still exploring their options in terms of their future career, who find the breadth of the programme appealing or who are interested in pursuing a career that is not represented in their school's CRS pathways. The CP supports students with clear career aspirations and/or a strong interest in a particular career field, or specialisation.

The Venn diagram below shows the similarities and differences between the CP and DP; this is a useful summary when talking to **stakeholders**. This shared understanding and common language will provide clarity and support for all educators working within an IB school offering both the DP and CP.

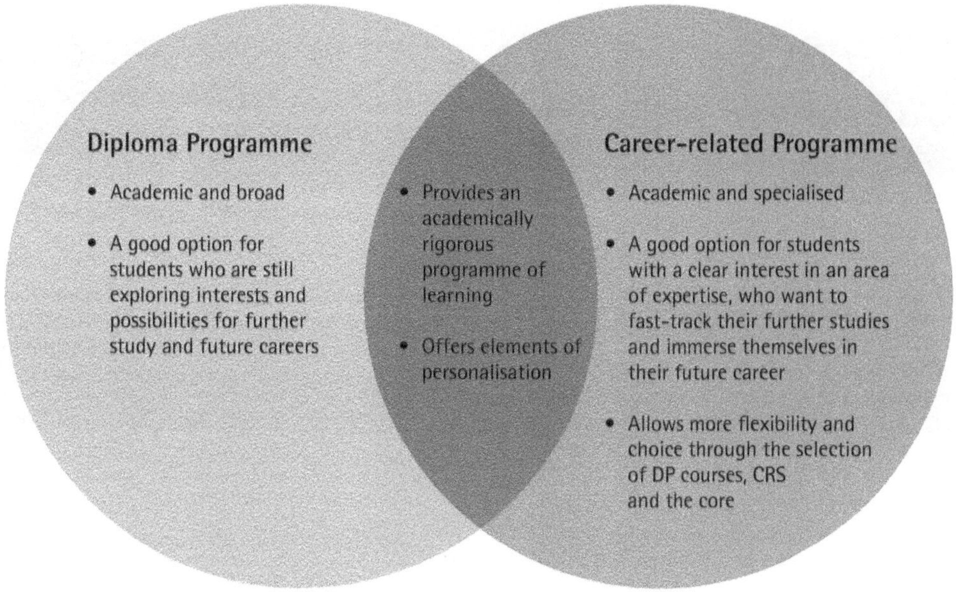

Top tip!

Note that university-provided CRS can enable CP graduates to be fast-tracked through their undergraduate studies by up to 18 months.

Personal and professional skills and the reflective project

PPS and the RP are critical components of the overall CP student experience. PPS acts as a central thread that weaves learning across all areas of the programme. The RP serves as a **culminating experience** that showcases the knowledge, skills and perspectives students have gained throughout their CP journey. Together, these two elements provide the strongest lens through which to explore and implement the CP Core.

These two components are intrinsically linked, as many skills developed through PPS will help prepare students for their RP. The RP itself is an excellent opportunity for students to apply what they have learned from their entire CP experience and showcase their growth in **critical thinking**, **ethical thinking**, communication and **intercultural understanding**.

Personal and professional skills

The PPS course has the potential to be incredibly impactful for both students and teachers.

- It is a taught component with a minimum commitment of 100 hours, although some schools allocate more than 240 hours to it. The number of hours you allocate will depend on the needs of your students, your staffing capacity, your timetable and your vision for your PPS course.
- The PPS course focuses on supporting students in developing skills that can be used across a variety of contexts.
- It is designed to help students thrive both personally and professionally after graduating from the CP.
- PPS is often described as the heart of the CP – the place where students can connect their learning as they inquire into their personal and professional development.
- The PPS component runs throughout a student's entire CP journey and should play an integral role in the successful implementation of the programme.

Reflective project

The RP is an exploration of an **ethical dilemma** within a career field of the student's choosing, culminating in an externally assessed academic research project that students can submit in a variety of formats.

- The RP is a fantastic opportunity for students to learn and apply vital skills for further study and employment while inquiring into an ethical dilemma highly relevant to their interests.
- Student voice and agency are central to the RP as students decide upon the career field, issue, ethical dilemma, research question, and how they want to present their work through one of the accepted formats.
- The RP can also be a useful tool for students in the university admissions process. Their work could be submitted as an example of their engagement with the area of their chosen undergraduate degree or could provide an interesting discussion point for any admissions interview.
- The RP is a component that should be introduced at the beginning of the CP journey and submitted within the second year of the programme.

The CP core components have been designed with intentional connections to ensure a holistic approach to student learning. The PPS and RP components are intrinsically linked, as much of the skill development that will take place in PPS will significantly benefit students in preparing for the RP. The RP is an excellent opportunity for students to apply what they have learned from their entire CP experience and showcase their growth in critical and ethical thinking, communication and intercultural understanding.

What do students say about their PPS experience?

Miyu's story:

"In Personal and Professional Skills (PPS), I love how open the conversation is. Getting to know everyone in my class more deeply has been enjoyable, and having the teacher participate in our discussions and debates has made it easier for me to express my thoughts in class. PPS has been useful for me in developing my ability to understand different perspectives and preparing me for the Reflective Project. PPS has impacted the way I observe the world around me, and I feel more prepared for my future career after taking this course."

Yun's story

"Personal and Professional Skills (PPS) is very different from other courses that I take. PPS encourages us to reflect deeply on ourselves, our values, our thinking, and our actions. The focus is not on content; rather, it is on me, the individual student, and my personal and professional development. Within PPS, I loved learning about intercultural understanding and applying this knowledge in both personal and professional contexts. I especially enjoyed exploring culture shock and reverse culture shock as I could relate to these feelings through my own experiences. I also loved the environment of PPS as it made me feel comfortable to share my thoughts with others and connect with people that I would not have interacted with as much outside of this class. PPS has been my bridge between academics, my personal life and my professional life, and has helped me understand myself and the world around me."

Commitment to success

Being part of the implementation of the CP is an opportunity to shape futures. The CP invites you to design personalised learning journeys that reflect your students' aspirations. Approach it with an entrepreneurial spirit and an innovative mindset. The flexibility of the CP framework empowers you to reimagine what education can look like. Lean into that agency!

Key takeaways: Chapter 1

- The CP is the perfect academic programme for students whose passions and strengths can be linked to a chosen career field.
- The CP is an academic equal to the DP.
- The PPS component can be described as a central point, where students can connect their learning
- The RP is a culminating, externally assessed academic research project that explores an ethical dilemma within a career field of the students' choosing.

Key terms

critical thinking: the process of examining a subject or idea carefully and critically, without allowing yourself to be influenced by opinions or feelings

culminating experience: a final academic requirement that demonstrates a student's mastery of the skills and knowledge they have acquired throughout the course

ethical dilemma: an ethical issue in which someone must choose between conflicting values or actions, each with its own drawbacks; while all ethical dilemmas are ethical issues, not all ethical issues necessarily present a dilemma

ethical thinking: the process of carefully considering right and wrong, and using your values to guide your decisions; this involves critically examining your own beliefs and the possible effects of choices on others to act responsibly and fairly

framework: a conceptual structure that organises thinking and provides contexts for understanding relationships between ideas

Higher Level (HL): a level in the Diploma Programme course, comprising a minimum of 240 timetabled hours

holistic: of or relating to a belief that different parts of something are interconnected and can only be explained by referring to the whole

intercultural understanding: the ability to recognise and respect cultural differences and interact effectively with people from different cultural backgrounds

stakeholder: a person, group or community that is affected by or has an interest in something; in the reflective project, this means everyone who might be impacted, whether they are in your own community or in other parts of the world

Standard Level (SL): a level in the Diploma Programme course, comprising a minimum of 150 timetabled hours

2 Staffing and timetabling of the Career-related Programme core

This chapter covers the following:

- Staffing models
- Effective practice in key roles
- Timetabling

This chapter is for Career-related Programme (CP) coordinators, personal and professional skills (PPS) coordinators/teachers and reflective project (RP) coordinators/supervisors.

Staffing models

The staffing and **timetabling** of the CP core varies widely from school to school, affected by:

- whether the school offers both the Diploma Programme (DP) and the CP, or if it exclusively offers the CP
- the levels of collaboration and integration between the DP and the CP at schools that offer both
- the number of chosen career-related studies (CRS) pathways
- whether the CRS pathways are school taught, delivered by external providers or a combination of both
- the number of students
- the number and expertise of staff
- the school-specific understanding of the role of the CP coordinator, DP coordinator or DP/CP coordinator and what is expected from that position.

There is no single way to correctly staff or timetable the CP core; all decisions have advantages and disadvantages. The context of your school will be the determining factor when making staffing and timetabling decisions.

Below are three examples of staffing structures for the CP core. Roles highlighted are required by the IB. All others are either an IB-recommended role or a role that exists in some CP schools, as it was deemed necessary in their staffing structure.

Example 1

School A: A small CP-only school

- CP coordinator, who is also the:
  - PPS teacher
  - RP coordinator
  - language and cultural studies (LCS) coordinator
  - community engagement (CE) coordinator

- RP supervisor(s)
- LCS teacher(s)
- CE advisor(s)

This example reflects a lean **staffing model**, where a few staff members cover all the required roles and responsibilities. In many cases, these staff members would also have responsibilities beyond delivering the CP. When coupled with externally delivered CRS options this can be a cost-effective way to offer the CP without increasing staff numbers.

Example 2

School B: A large CP-only school

- CP coordinator
- PPS coordinator
- PPS teacher(s)
- RP coordinator
- RP supervisors
- LCS coordinator
- LCS teacher(s)
- LCS mentors (IB-recommended)
- CE coordinator
- CE adviser(s)
- CE mentor(s) (IB-recommended)

This example reflects a school with a much larger cohort of CP students than School A. Due to the larger cohorts, staff roles and responsibilities need to be more spread out to make the jobs manageable and to allow staff to be effective in their roles. In this example, the IB-recommended roles can be afforded and justified in addition to the IB-required roles due to the scale of the programme and the number of students involved. The PPS coordinator is a role that exists in some large CP schools; this can be helpful when there are multiple sections of the PPS course, and the CP coordinator has several responsibilities and is potentially involved in leading other aspects of the school.

Example 3

School C: A mid-sized DP/CP school

- DP/CP coordinator, who is also the:
  - PPS teacher
- extended essay (EE)/RP coordinator
- EE/RP supervisors
- theory of knowledge (TOK) coordinator
- TOK teacher(s)
- LCS coordinator
- LCS teacher(s)
- creativity, activity, service (CAS)/CE coordinator
- CAS/CE adviser(s)

This example reflects a DP/CP school where the DP/CP coordinator takes a more active role in delivering the personal and professional skills course, while delegating and managing the coordinators of the other DP/CP core components. The core component(s) that the DP/CP coordinator is more directly involved in may vary, depending on their expertise and capacity. As the role of DP/CP coordinator may come with additional leadership responsibilities in school, it is not unusual for that staff member to be removed entirely from responsibility for the delivery of each component so they can instead focus more on supporting the various core component coordinators, who actively implement the individual core components.

The examples of staffing structures above are just a snapshot of the many possible structures for staffing the core in CP schools. There are also schools with independent DP and CP coordinators, and with the DP and CP core staffed completely separately. There is no right or wrong regarding these decisions, as long as all the positions required by the IB guidance documents are in place.

Effective practice in key roles

The key roles for staffing the PPS and the RP components are the optional PPS coordinator/lead teacher, PPS teacher(s), RP coordinator and RP supervisor(s). Depending on your school's size and structure, some of these roles may be held by the same person.

You can find clear descriptions of all roles and responsibilities in the respective IB guidance documents.

Here, we will explore what effective practice can look like for these crucial roles in implementing the CP core.

Personal and professional skills coordinator/lead teacher

The PPS coordinator or lead teacher role may exist within your school or be designated as part of the CP coordinator role. Regardless of title, the person in this role is responsible for designing an effective PPS course and ensuring it is taught and implemented to the highest standards.

An effective PPS coordinator/lead teacher should:

- ✓ lead and collaborate with other educators when planning instruction and assessments based on IB documentation
- ✓ demonstrate excellent communication and interpersonal skills while working with fellow educators, students and the wider school community
- ✓ collaborate with all CP core component coordinators to ensure a coherent implementation of all components
- ✓ collaborate with the staff who plan and deliver the school curricula for pastoral care, wellbeing and university and career counselling, to ensure any crossover with PPS is planned for and intentional
- ✓ have an excellent working relationship with the school librarian, as they can play a key role in the delivery of both the PPS and RP components
- ✓ engage with students and parents/guardians to inform the planning and delivery of the PPS curriculum
- ✓ engage with external stakeholders to explore opportunities to enrich the PPS component within the school
- ✓ support DP subject teachers and the CRS teaching team/providers with integrating PPS into their respective subjects
- ✓ support PPS teachers in developing their ability to plan in collaboration with students
- ✓ support PPS teachers in developing their ability to mentor CP students, especially during student-led or student-created inquiries
- ✓ support PPS teachers in cultivating a classroom culture that allows for open dialogue and complete trust when discussing sensitive issues
- ✓ collaborate with DP core staff, particularly the theory of knowledge teaching team, to look for potential collaboration opportunities when working in a DP/CP school
- ✓ be active in the CP community to share effective practice and learn from and alongside other CP schools.

Personal and professional skills teacher

Teaching PPS can be a unique experience. Within the framework and learning outcomes provided, educators have the autonomy to plan inquiries with and for their students based on student needs and aspirations. PPS should be tailored and personalised for each cohort and student. This level of autonomy and personalisation may seem daunting to begin with, but teaching PPS and being part of a course that brings so much growth to students is extremely rewarding. This book will provide you with example processes, guidance and inquiries to support you in your PPS planning and implementation.

When considering effective practice, PPS teachers should:

- ✓ build excellent working relationships with their students by taking the time to get to know them and support them in setting personal and professional development goals
- ✓ maintain an active interest in their students' progress in their other studies, to help them connect their learning throughout their PPS inquiries and to do more research into areas they find interesting or need to progress within
- ✓ make time for planning inquiries with students and support them in creating their own inquiries
- ✓ set clear rules for debates and discussions in collaboration with students – this is especially important when discussing more sensitive topics
- ✓ upskill their knowledge and understanding of the CRS pathways within their class, where possible; this will improve their ability to mentor their students through the lens of their future career field
- ✓ understand that they will facilitate learning through **mentoring** and coaching their PPS students
- ✓ be knowledgeable in all four CP core components to make appropriate connections throughout PPS
- ✓ hone their ability to ask thought-provoking questions that can guide reflective and **reflexive** thinking in their students
- ✓ see their students as young professionals in their chosen career fields, understanding that the role of the PPS teacher is to support students in developing the skills required to be personally content and professionally successful.

Top tip!

Many CP coordinators like to be heavily involved in the delivery of PPS. It is a fantastic way to get to know students better and provide more personalised guidance throughout their learning journey!

Reflective project coordinator

The RP coordinator role is pivotal in supporting the successful culmination of the CP core. RP coordinators must harness the skill development and exploration of **ethics** in PPS lessons and across the CP core to prepare students for this extended independent academic research project.

An effective RP coordinator should:

- ✓ work closely with all CP core coordinators and teachers to understand when related skills, content and concepts are being delivered in each component; this helps them create the optimal timeline so students progress in the RP at a rate appropriate to their knowledge and skill development
- ✓ have an excellent working relationship with the school librarian, who can play a key role in the delivery of both the RP and PPS components
- ✓ have a solid understanding of ethics and ethical thinking
- ✓ have a passion for ethical discussions and debates – they will frequently have to provide thought-provoking questions when supporting students, RP supervisors and PPS teachers in examining potential ethical dilemmas and evaluating different perspectives on ethical dilemmas
- ✓ have a general understanding of the CRS pathways on offer
- ✓ be knowledgeable about processes for evaluating source selection and identifying bias
- ✓ support RP supervisors in mentoring their students by helping them understand how to give high quality written and verbal feedback
- ✓ work with RP supervisors and the PPS teaching team to create a robust process that helps students to develop the most appropriate research question for their chosen ethical dilemma
- ✓ create a **moderation process** that ensures accurate and reliable feedback and marking (see 'Top tip' below)
- ✓ upskill RP supervisors in ethics, the CRS pathways on offer within the school and any chosen career fields within each CP cohort
- ✓ establish a connection with the CRS teaching team/providers so they can assist students in their RP journey
- ✓ work alongside a standalone DP EE coordinator (if that position exists within the school) to ensure that EE and RP supervisors are selected with staff expertise and quality of student experience in mind.

Top tip!

Although the RP is externally assessed, it is still essential to moderate the feedback given by supervisors to ensure consistency and best practice for all students. The moderation process may also be necessary for determining predicted grades. More information on the moderation process is provided in Chapter 11.

Reflective project supervisor

The role of the RP supervisor can be complex. They are tasked with supporting their student(s) in exploring complicated ethical dilemmas within a professional context that could be unfamiliar to the supervisor. They may also be supporting multiple learners in producing RPs in a range of different formats.

RP supervisors are not expected to have extensive knowledge about each ethical dilemma or chosen format for the RP; their role is to facilitate and guide students through the process, helping them to access the appropriate support and stakeholders at the right moments.

While this can seem daunting, the role of the RP supervisor is a great opportunity to connect with students through an area of interest in which they are deeply engaged and about which they are genuinely passionate. Supporting students in this extended academic project can be incredibly interesting and rewarding.

When considering effective practice, RP supervisors should:

- ✓ engage fully with each student regarding their chosen career field, ethical dilemma and research question
- ✓ take an interest in their student's holistic education to help foster an effective working relationship
- ✓ establish protocols for communication that are effective and efficient in collaboration with their students and according to school norms
- ✓ understand that it is not their role to teach or instruct, but to give feedback and guide students to the resources they need at the appropriate times, and to provide students with questions or reframe them as needed to help them overcome challenges
- ✓ become familiar with the CRS pathways offered in their school, as this will support them in their role
- ✓ form a support network with their student(s) consisting of, but not limited to, their PPS teacher, their CRS provider, the librarian, and other resources the school can utilise such as the CP core and DP teachers, and external CRS mentors
- ✓ engage with the wider CP community to share effective practice and learn from others in the same role in different schools and contexts
- ✓ contribute to the school moderation protocols to ensure best practice in giving feedback, marking and predicting grades.

Top tip!

As a RP supervisor, being genuinely interested and curious will not only help your students, but it will also increase their enjoyment of the RP journey.

The role of the librarian

When discussing the staffing of the PPS and RP components, the role of the librarian deserves a special mention. As with all staffing decisions, school context is key. In some schools, the librarian will have little involvement in the DP and/or CP core provision. In others, the librarian will arguably be the most impactful member of the DP and/or CP core staff.

Librarians may be the staff members who are best-equipped to support student inquiries and project-based learning as, unlike some subject teachers, they do not approach each inquiry through the lens of their respective subject or discipline. When this unique approach is coupled with a skill set that may include - but is not limited to - expertise in academic research, referencing, academic integrity, **source curation** and selection, identifying bias, the ethical use of AI, and effective communication in academic writing, the librarian can quickly become the most valuable person on the DP and/or CP core staff.

Reflection

Reflect on the following questions about staffing. Discuss any that are of particular interest to you with the rest of the CP core team within your school.

- How do your current PPS and RP **staffing models** support your implementation of these components?
- Thinking about the suggestions for effective practice shared in this chapter, where can you identify effective practice within your current PPS and RP provision?
- Is your school fully utilising the expertise of its staff and the wider school community to enhance its PPS and RP components? Can you identify any untapped expertise?
- Within the bounds of possibility, considering staff capacity and school finances, are there any changes in your school's CP core staffing model that you would advocate for? If so, what are they, and what impact do you hope these changes will have on student experience?

Timetabling

Timetabling can be a complex job at the best of times, but when you begin to include courses from different exam boards, external providers, and perhaps multiple IB programmes for your students aged 16–19, that level of complexity can increase dramatically. Whether your school follows a Week A/Week B schedule, an eight-day rotating schedule, 4×4 blocks or a more traditional five-day fixed timetable, timetabling considerations always have the potential to either magnify or impinge on the effectiveness of your school's educational offering.

Reflection

Review the following questions with the appropriate colleagues to stimulate discussions that will lead to the ideal timetabling structure for your school context.

- How many hours will be dedicated to the PPS, LCS, and CE components?
- How will staff be selected to fulfil these hours – by available capacity or by how well-suited they are to the role?
- Do you have an appropriate job description for each role, considering IB guidance and what effective practice looks like?
- Does the RP coordinator require designated time to work with students? If so, when does this happen?
- Does the CP core team have time to meet and plan? Is this considered in your timetable?
- If input from the librarian is planned for, when does this occur?

If you are working in a DP/CP school:

- Will the DP and CP coordinator positions be combined?
- Will the EE and RP coordinator positions be combined?
- Will the CAS coordinator and the CE coordinator positions be combined?
- If so, what timetable considerations need to happen to allow the staff in these dual roles to be successful and available to both their DP and CP students at the appropriate times?
- Will staff supervise the EE *and* the RP, or will there be separate supervisors for each?
- Will theory of knowledge be blocked against PPS, or will PPS be timetabled for the same block of time as a commonly unchosen DP subject group that allows staff sharing across these core components?
- Will the LCS coordinator position be standalone, part of the CP coordinator role or combined with another role within the school, such as Faculty or Department Head of Languages?

Timetabling best practice

Consider your ideals for each component before the practicalities of timetabling.

Decide on the optimal number of hours for PPS, LCS, and CE when you have a clear vision of everything you want to achieve through each component.

Make the rationale for proposals very clear in terms of impact on students when communicating them with senior leadership.

As far as possible, select staff by fit for the role rather than available capacity for the hours.

Identify key staff who can positively impact your CP core provision and do what you can with the timetable to allow them to be involved. For example, if you identify a potentially fantastic PPS teacher, who is not available when your school currently blocks PPS, consider blocking PPS against a DP subject group that your CP students do not commonly take. This might free up that member of staff to join the CP core team without impacting any other area of the timetable.

When planned for appropriately, an increased number of hours from the stated 100 minimum in PPS can be extremely valuable to the comprehensiveness and quality of the CP core.

A DP school can add the CP to their offerings with no increase in full-time staff count by combining coordinator positions across the programmes and choosing external providers for its CRS options.

Empower CP core staff to be ambassadors for the programme within the school community. The CP is still relatively new worldwide compared to the DP, and misconceptions can arise easily. Knowledgeable CP ambassadors might even include CP alumni or Year 2 students, and can be vital to the success of the programme.

Top tip!

It is possible to combine PPS Year 1 and Year 2 students in the same class if the teacher is experienced in supporting students through inquiries and project-based learning. While not an optimal approach, this could allow smaller schools to reduce their staffing.

Commitment to success

The strength of the CP core lies not just in its components, but in the people who bring them to life. Staffing and timetabling decisions shape the daily experience of students; getting them right is an act of leadership. See each staffing and scheduling choice as an opportunity to elevate the student experience. Invest in the people, systems and structures that will inspire confidence, collaboration and continuity across the CP.

Key takeaways: Chapter 2

- There is no one-size-fits-all model for staffing and timetabling the CP core. Provision should reflect your school's context.
- Combining DP and CP core roles is possible, but this must be well-planned to avoid overburdening staff.
- PPS and RP staff should be collaborative, reflective and connected to the wider CP core team.
- Librarians can be key contributors to the PPS course and the RP due to their expertise in academic research and writing.
- Timetabling decisions should prioritise pedagogical goals over convenience, with strategic planning to enable the most suitable staff to be involved in the areas where they can be most impactful.

Key terms

ethics: moral beliefs, rules and principles about right and wrong

mentoring: the process of helping or giving advice to a younger or less experienced colleague

moderation process: a school-based system for reviewing and aligning feedback, grades and the consistency of the student experience

source curation: the selection, gathering and presentation of the most useful and relevant sources and information for a particular topic

staffing models: sample structures showing how schools of varying size and complexity assign roles based on available personnel and resources

timetabling: the process of allocating hours and scheduling staff with a strategic vision to create the optimal conditions for teaching and learning

3 Involving key stakeholders

This chapter covers the following:

- Identifying key stakeholders
- Involving key stakeholders in personal and professional skills
- Involving key stakeholders in the reflective project

This chapter is intended for all staff involved in the implementation of the Career-related Programme (CP) core, particularly CP coordinators, personal and professional skills (PPS) coordinators and teachers, and reflective project (RP) coordinators and supervisors.

Identifying key stakeholders

Identifying and leaning into the expertise and perspectives of key stakeholders in the CP core can elevate the student experience across all core components. Involving key stakeholders at the right point in the process – planning, delivery or assessment – will have a big impact on the core's quality and effectiveness.

The following groups could be considered key stakeholders in the implementation of the CP core (although this list is not exhaustive).

Stakeholder group	Examples
External stakeholders	• **External experts** (locally or globally) • **Industry leads** • External CRS providers • Other CP schools (regionally or internationally)
School community-based stakeholders	• Parents • CP alumni • Local CRS providers • Other CP schools (locally)
School-based stakeholders	• **CP core teaching team** • Students • DP teachers • Librarian • In-school CRS teachers • Pastoral and wellbeing leads • University and college counselling team

This chapter looks at how these groups can contribute to the PPS and RP components of the programme. They will appear again throughout this resource with advice on how to best harness their expertise within the CP core.

Reflection

Within your own school context, there may be other stakeholders who are crucial to the successful implementation of the CP core. Reflect on this with the CP core teaching team at your school using the following questions.

- Beyond the list at the start of this chapter, who else could be identified as a key stakeholder and what unique expertise and perspectives can they offer?
- What impact would their involvement have on your students' experience?
- What do you need to make this happen? (Planning time? Financial resources? Time to network and create partnerships?)

Involving key stakeholders in personal and professional skills

The PPS course provides the perfect opportunity to harness positive influence and impact from a wide range of stakeholders.

The CP core teaching team

The core components of the CP have been designed with collaboration and integration in mind, and a collaboratively planned CP core can be far more impactful than implementing each component in isolation. Effective collaboration among the CP core teaching team will provide your students with a holistic experience and avoid overlaps in their learning.

The early PPS inquiries in the first year of the CP (CP 1) are a good example of what a positive outcome of collaboration among the CP core teaching team may look like. These inquiries can be designed to expand on and link together student learning in the introductory unit of the language and cultural studies (LCS) component and the introduction and orientation of community engagement (CE). Coordinating on the design of these inquiries is a great way to show students the interconnectedness of the CP core and how development within these three components will better prepare them for success in the RP.

Top tip!

Try to schedule regular meetings for the CP core teaching team. Many schools already do this for subject, faculty, department or year-level teams to ensure consistency and coherence in planning, delivery and assessment.

Students

Much like the broader concept and purpose of the CP, the PPS course is student-centred by design. Because it is student centered, it is recommended that students be engaged in the following ways:

- as key stakeholders in the planning process, which can make the course more relevant to their aspirations and needs.
- in the delivery of the course, as this will allow them to take ownership of their own learning by creating and leading their own inquiries.
- in the assessment processes, as this can inform decisions over assessment methodology and support PPS teachers in finding the best and most innovative ways to assess student growth towards the learning outcomes.

CP alumni

If your school has already produced CP graduates, engage your alumni to share their feedback on their CP core experience. This can be a deeply impactful exercise, helping the CP core teaching team to identify both the strengths and areas that may need further development in how the CP core is implemented.

Feedback from CP alumni can lead to...

- ...changing the sequencing of the course.
- ...changing the amount of time dedicated to a particular inquiry.
- ...adapting the content used to explore learning outcomes.
- ...re-evaluating the assessment methods used at the end of an inquiry.
- ...identifying misconceptions students have about the PPS course and how it connects with other CP core components.
- ...identifying the most impactful learning experiences for students and making the best use of those in future iterations of the course.
- ...revisiting the guidance used to support students in curating their **portfolios.**

Another way to leverage the expertise of CP alumni is through a **mentoring** programme for current students – perhaps pairing alumni with students working on the same career-related study. It is, of course, important to have a clear structure for the mentoring sessions so that both parties gain something from the process and feel it is an effective use of their time. Implemented well, this kind of programme can be a positive experience for both students and alumni.

Top tip!

If you are in a school that is new to the CP, consider reaching out to more experienced CP schools within your network to see if they would be willing to share feedback they have received from their CP alumni. This could accelerate your learning and support your implementation of the core as a new CP school.

Parents

Involving the parents of CP students in the planning process provides PPS teachers with another way to get to know the students entering their CP cohorts and to recognise their aspirations, goals and needs within the curriculum. While parent involvement should be managed carefully in terms of the clarity of communication around the purpose of their involvement, inviting parents to be partners in designing and implementing the CP core can prove helpful in creating a bespoke PPS course for each cohort and student.

Another way to engage the parent community and to leverage their expertise as key stakeholders is to consider what they can directly offer to the PPS experience, such as providing expert input. For example, you might reach out to a parent who works in international business and ask them to host a workshop or series of seminars on cross-cultural communication and its importance in the business world. This could provide real-world examples and a depth of learning that would enhance the overall impact of a particular inquiry and improve the student experience within PPS.

Diploma Programme teachers

Diploma Programme (DP) teachers play a more important role in the CP core than they may realise. Those who are used to working in a DP-only school are usually aware of their responsibility to include and reference the DP core components within their subjects; however, unless they have experience working in a CP-only or DP/CP school, they may not make connections with the CP core components within their DP subjects.

In a DP/CP school, much of the responsibility for establishing an equitable of connection between the DP and CP core components rests with the CP coordinator and the CP core teaching team, who must ensure that their DP colleagues are knowledgeable about the CP core offered within their school. This supports CP students in understanding the interconnectedness of the three-part educational framework that makes up the CP. It also provides parity for CP students with their DP peers in their experience of DP subjects. All this can significantly influence the perception of the CP within DP/CP schools. Involving DP teachers in the planning, delivery and assessment of CP core components can take this a step further and help them become more effective teachers for the CP students in their classes.

Career-related studies teachers and providers

As you have seen, specialists such as career-related studies (CRS) teachers and providers can provide expertise and learning opportunities that enhance the PPS experience. This can be particularly impactful during inquiries that focus on contexts within CRS and professional life. For example, you could invite all CRS teachers and providers to support and assess students as part of an inquiry that focuses on workplace readiness and developing communication skills for use during offline and online interviews. CRS teachers and providers can also mentor students in the specific context of their future careers, as the PPS teacher guides them through more general interview preparations and identifies good practices that apply to all offline and online interviews.

Inviting CRS teachers and providers to be involved in the delivery and assessment processes maximises the benefit to CP students as they receive better support in preparation for an assessment and more actionable and specific feedback after the assessment.

External experts and industry leads

External experts and industry leads can be utilised in a similar way to parent and teacher and provider stakeholders. However, your school may not have an existing relationship with this group, so there is more detailed information on the power of networking in relation to the PPS course in Chapter 4.

Pastoral and wellbeing leads and the university and college counselling team

Despite the name we have given to this stakeholder group, it is challenging to identify all the people who may be involved here, as staffing structures in these areas can vary significantly from school to school. For example, much of the CP core content is explored through the lens of a student's own cultural identity, ethics, morals, values, career aspirations and personal skill development, so in your own school context, this stakeholder may be the person or department responsible for any work in these areas that is already underway. They can play an important part in helping to design the PPS course and the wider CP core, to recognise and celebrate prior learning.

You can also involve other knowledgeable members of staff from different areas of the school to support the CP core teaching team. This support can flow throughout the planning, delivery and assessment processes. The staff responsible for the prior learning could become key members of the CP core teaching team or contribute occasionally by leading on areas where their expertise can bring value to the student experience.

Other CP schools

Building connections with other CP schools can enrich the PPS experience for both staff and students. For schools newer to the CP, these partnerships offer valuable opportunities for shared learning and support. Consider collaborating on curriculum planning and involving students from each school in shared activities, such as debates. Initiatives like these foster professional dialogue, broaden perspectives and strengthen the CP community across schools.

Involving key stakeholders in the reflective project

The same collaborative and student-centred approach is essential for enhancing the quality and impact of students' learning experiences in the RP.

RP coordinators, supervisors and students can benefit from the expertise, perspectives and support of a diverse group of stakeholders throughout this learning journey.

The CP core teaching team

Many of the foundational skills necessary for the RP – research, intercultural understanding, creative and critical thinking, and reflective and **reflexive** thinking – are supported and developed through the learning experiences guided by teachers in the CP core.

Language and cultural studies

This component helps students to expand their linguistic and cultural repertoires and experiences. By creating their own language and cultural portraits, students develop a much deeper understanding of themselves and appreciate diverse perspectives from different language and cultural backgrounds and contexts. This also helps them develop their reflexivity and self-awareness by thinking about and evaluating how their personal biases and values are formed, and how different perspectives can also be valid.

Community engagement

CE teachers can help students connect with community members and discover opportunities to engage with them in dialogic, reciprocal, reflective and reflexive ways. This expands their understanding from a personal to a relational to a systems dimension, fostering critical, social, affective and ethical thinking skills. These skills help students gain a deeper understanding of local and global issues and develop the ability to manage complexity and reflect on their thinking and values to determine and justify their own positionality.

Personal and professional skills

PPS teachers prepare students by exposing them to different ethical principles and enhancing their conceptual understanding. PPS also helps students develop a variety of skills, including research, analysis and reflective/reflexive practice. Students should also be exposed to different text types, which will familiarise them with a variety of stylistic conventions. As they curate **artefacts** for their portfolios, students learn to analyse, synthesise and link evidence to demonstrate their understanding across their entire learning experience.

Integrative culminating experience

As you can see from the graphic below, the RP functions as the integrative culminating experience for the CP core. Each of the four core components provides distinct yet complementary skill sets that students draw upon when completing their RP.

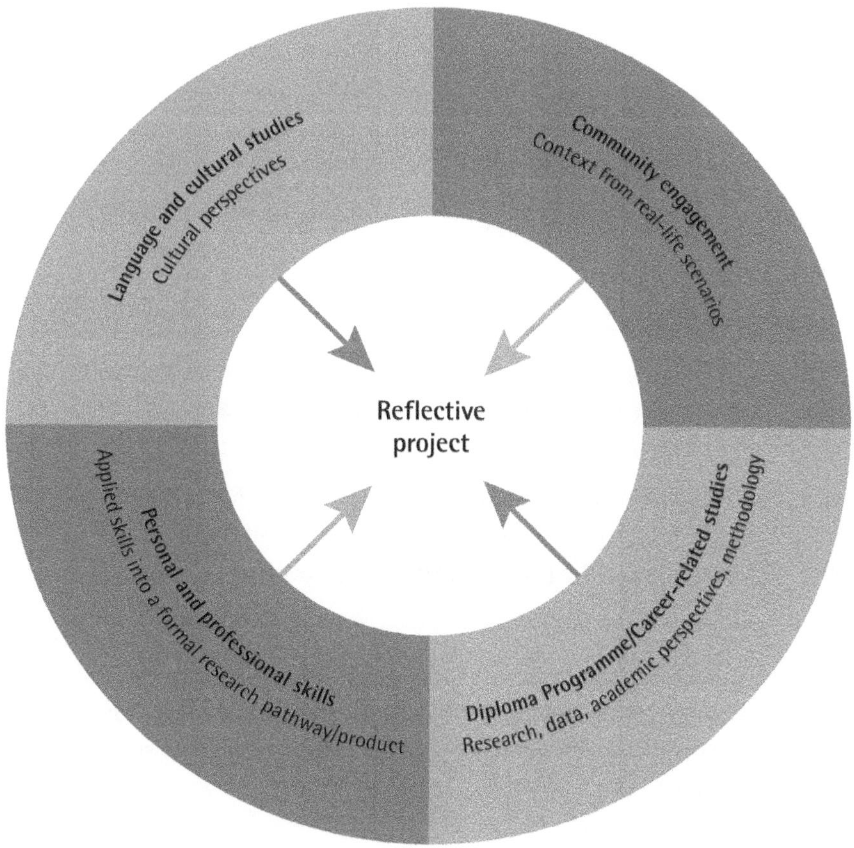

For more information on how the RP is supported by other components of the CP core, see Chapter 11.

Students

Although the RP is a student's self-directed, independent process, feedback still plays a crucial role in their learning journey, and schools are encouraged to organise opportunities for students to give and receive both peer and supervisor feedback. While supervisors support students for three to six hours in total, peer discussions can be facilitated to help students explore ideas at several different points throughout the process.

It may also be beneficial for students to have peer discussions on current progress and thinking during the preparation and planning phase. During the presentation phase, students can engage with each other to provide feedback on research plans, quality, inclusion of required elements, and the effectiveness of the organisation and communication of research findings and analysis.

In addition, you could also organise Year 2 CP students to be RP mentors for Year 1 CP students. For example, CP 1 students could attend CP 2 students' presentations (if this works with your school's timeline, of course), as a form of induction to the process and the research methodology involved.

CP alumni

CP alumni can be excellent mentors throughout students' RP journey. They can provide useful tips and suggestions on the entire process, from identifying ethical dilemmas to research resources, methods and research analysis. They can also be valuable interviewees if the CP alumni and the student share the same career interest or research topic.

Parents

Parents can contribute to the RP journey in several ways. They can:

- be mentors, guiding students on ethical issues and **applied ethics** in their respective career fields
- provide historical background or contexts for the ethical dilemma the student is researching
- be primary sources for students' research topics, offering a perspective on the ethical dilemma as stakeholder representatives via surveys, questionnaires or one-on-one interviews.

Diploma Programme teachers

DP teachers are often also RP supervisors, especially in schools with both programmes. The RP timeline may be synchronised with the **extended essay (EE)** timeline to make it easier to coordinate and implement.

It is helpful to pair students with subject teachers who have some knowledge and expertise in the student's selected career fields – for example, an Arts and Design teacher could supervise a student whose RP focuses on an ethical dilemma in that field, or a Physics teacher could supervise a student whose RP topic was in aviation and aeronautics. However, it is even more important for supervisors to be skilled in guiding and supporting students throughout the RP process, regardless of their expertise in a specific field. The supervisor should be seen as a co-learner with the student on their RP learning journey.

The primary role of the supervisor is to provide timely feedback and help the student navigate the process of project management. The RP focuses on an ethical dilemma, analysis of the research, effective communication of research findings, and the student's personal position on the dilemma with evidence-based justification. Students should be given guidance on:

- specific research areas
- best methods for analysis
- effective communication formats
- ethical frameworks or theories that may assist them in reaching personal conclusions.

If a supervisor lacks expertise in a specific area, they can encourage students to engage with other members of the school community, and this is where DP teachers can play their part. For instance, students interested in creating a documentary could be directed to the school's Film and Media teacher; those investigating the effects of gaming on children could speak to a Psychology teacher.

Although the RP is externally assessed, supervisors are required to provide a predicted grade. Many schools engage in a standardisation practice with their RP supervisors to generate more cohesive and accurate predicted grades (see chapter 11 for more information). There are two main ways to do this:

- read and mark the project to decide on a predicted grade, or
- use the RP **qualitative grade descriptors** to determine achievement level quality.

Whichever option you choose, this is a great way to familiarise supervisors with the RP assessment criteria so they can better guide their students. This can also be a great training opportunity for any new RP supervisors, to explain the requirements of the RP and explore ways of guiding students to the best possible outcomes.

Career-related studies teachers and providers

Depending on how your school offers the CRS component, CRS teachers are another potential source of student support. If the CRS is internally delivered by the school – for example, by using Advanced Placement (AP) or Business and Technology Education Council (BTEC) as your CRS – the teachers of those courses can serve as RP supervisors.

If your school works with an external provider, such as the Savannah College of Art and Design (SCAD) or the Sustainability Management School Switzerland (SUMAS), or with an industry provider such as the World Academy of Sport (WAoS), their teachers can serve as mentors.

Students could interview their CRS teachers and mentors – many of whom are active practitioners in their fields – to gain a deeper understanding of the historical context, impacted stakeholders and societal trends linked to their ethical dilemma.

You can reach out to your CRS providers at the beginning of the preparation and planning phase to ask them to provide a workshop or information session featuring applied ethics and common ethical issues in their fields of work or relevant industries. Your school's CRS providers can also provide valuable CE opportunities for your students, through which they can discover real-world ethical issues and dilemmas that can be the focus of a RP.

External experts and industry leads

Establishing connections with external experts and industry leads expands the range of perspectives and resources available to students. These people may be drawn from your school's parent body or from community members. These individuals or organisations can be great sources of information for students to gather primary sources or gain deeper insight into ethical issues and dilemmas within those industries. Similarly, they can provide opportunities for CE or projects that can guide students towards appropriate ethical dilemmas.

Pastoral and wellbeing leads and the university and college counselling team

The RP is a lengthy and challenging project that requires careful planning and good self-management skills. Some students might require pastoral support to help them develop these skills and to guide them if they start to feel overwhelmed by the task – for example, if things are not progressing as well as they would like, or if the outcome deviates from their expectations.

The RP can also be useful for students in the university admissions process. Their work could be submitted as an example of their engagement with the area of their chosen undergraduate degree, or it could be an interesting discussion point for an admissions interview. Your school's university and college counselling team can provide guidance and counselling services to aid the process and make students' RP even more impactful and relevant for their future learning and career progression.

Other CP schools

If there are other CP schools nearby, consider forming partnerships with them and connecting your CP students with theirs. This can be particularly beneficial for schools that are new to the programme. Your school's CP coordinator or RP coordinator could even organise a cross-school standardisation practice or invite students from other schools to join the oral presentation stage of your students' RP journey.

Commitment to success

Successful implementation of the CP does not happen in isolation. Involving key stakeholders builds a shared sense of purpose and is pivotal in leveraging expertise to maximise the positive impact of the CP in your school. When people feel heard and involved, they are more likely to contribute meaningfully. Seek out diverse voices, invite authentic input and treat collaboration as a cornerstone of your implementation process. The strength of the CP grows with every partnership you cultivate.

Key takeaways: Chapter 3

- Involving a range of stakeholders can enhance the student CP experience, in the contexts of PPS and the RP.
- Collaboration within the CP core team ensures a connected learning experience in each core component.
- Students should help shape all aspects of the PPS course and demonstrate deep engagement with their chosen RP issue and ethical dilemma.
- CP alumni can offer valuable feedback and mentorship.
- External experts can enrich PPS and RP inquiries with real-world insights.
- DP and CRS teachers can support contextual and academic integration throughout the CP.
- It is helpful to identify the good work that may already exist in your school and recognise prior and concurrent learning in your PPS course.
- It is also important to leverage the variety of expertise and perspectives that exist within your school to support students through their RP journey.

Key terms

applied ethics: the branch of ethics that focuses on how ethical theories and principles can be used to address real-world ethical questions

artefact: a curated piece of evidence that can be used to demonstrate progress against one or more of the PPS learning outcomes

CP core teaching team: the staff responsible for delivering the four CP core components: personal and professional skills (PPS), the reflective project (RP), language and cultural studies (LCS) and community engagement (CE)

external experts and **industry leads:** professionals from outside the school who can offer specialised knowledge and/or real-world experience relevant to personal and professional skills and the reflective project

extended essay (EE): a component of the DP core that requires students to embark on an independent, self-directed piece of academic research, developing skills in academic writing, time management and critical thinking

portfolio: a curated collection of student work showing growth, reflection and achievement across all personal and professional skills outcomes

qualitative grade descriptors: detailed written statements that define the characteristics of student performance at each grade level (A–E) for assessment purposes; these are used by supervisors or coordinators to evaluate student work against standardised benchmarks and generate predicted grades based on the quality and depth of demonstrated skills rather than numerical scores

reflexive: able to examine your own thoughts, feelings, beliefs, attitudes and behaviours; in the context of the CP Core, it means being aware of your own assumptions and biases, and understanding how these influence your responses and decisions

4 Professional development and networking

This chapter covers the following:

- Professional development for Career-related Programme core staff
- The importance of networking

This chapter is intended for all staff involved in the implementation of the Career-related Programme (CP).

Professional development for Career-related Programme core staff

Whether you are new to the CP or an experienced CP practitioner, accessing impactful and personalised professional development is crucial for your growth as an educator. It also plays an important part in how you positively influence the student experience within your school. This section focuses on questions that can help you and the broader CP core teaching team to identify strengths and areas for professional development. They are designed to enhance your overall CP core provision.

Top tip!

The professional development suggestions here should be considered complementary to the IB requirements for workshop completion and successful authorisation/evaluation to deliver or continue delivering the CP.

The following questions are designed to encourage personal reflection on your readiness for your role(s) in the CP core. These questions will help you identify your strengths, areas for development and the support you can offer to colleagues. They will also guide you on how to access the most suitable professional development within and outside your school.

- After reviewing the IB guide(s) and the examples of effective practice provided in Chapter 2, what are your initial impressions of the roles and responsibilities you will assume?
- How would you describe your current feelings about these responsibilities? Excited and optimistic? Apprehensive and nervous? Somewhere in between?
- Based on your current understanding of your roles and responsibilities, what skills do you possess that will enable you to be an effective practitioner? For example: 'I am experienced in leading coaching conversations, and I believe this will support me in my roles as a personal and professional skills

teacher and reflective project supervisor. I should be able to use this skill to better get to know my students and provide thought-provoking interactions that support their growth and development through both components.'

- Do you think developing this skill would also be beneficial for CP core team members in other roles? Would you feel comfortable leading in-school professional development for your colleagues in this area?
- Are there any aspects of your role(s) that you feel underprepared for or inexperienced in? For example: 'I have not taught intercultural understanding before, and I am worried about being able to support a multi-cultural classroom in exploring intercultural understanding together. My students are quite diverse in terms of their cultural identities. I am concerned about conversations leading to people getting offended if I do not manage them in the right way.'
- Who can you identify in your school who would be excellent at the aspects of the role you feel underprepared for or inexperienced in? What makes you think they would be good in this area?
- Can they support you by becoming directly involved and sharing their expertise?
- Would they also be able to provide you with in-school professional development to enhance your confidence and experience in this area?
- What other external professional development opportunities can you identify that would help you become more effective in your role?
- What impact do you think engaging in this professional development would have on your CP students?
- What do you need to access your chosen professional development? Funding? Release time from school? Is there a process to apply for this? If not, who do you reach out to?

The personal reflection questions should help you:

✓ process your thoughts about your current role(s) and responsibilities

✓ identify your strengths and what support you can offer to your colleagues

✓ identify your areas for development and where you can find support in school

✓ research and identify impactful and personalised professional development whilst being able to articulate the value of engaging in this with reference directly to the CP student experience

✓ plan your next steps in applying for the appropriate external professional development within your school context.

The following questions will support the CP core teaching team members in recognising expertise within the school and leveraging that to upskill all CP core staff. They will also help identify gaps in desired knowledge and skills, and focus efforts on identifying appropriate external professional development opportunities.

- Considering the personal reflection questions, what expertise do individuals within the team have that can be shared through in-school professional development?
- Can you identify common themes in the areas you have identified as needing development?
- Are there any individuals or groups within the school outside of the CP core teaching team who have the skills to support you in improving in these areas?

- If not, could these issues be addressed by external professional development?
- If so, would it be beneficial for the whole team to participate in each external professional development opportunity, or will you send only one member of the team to each, allowing you to address more of your needs with the available resources?
- Could those attending external professional development then host in-school workshops for the wider team to share their learning?

These discussion questions are intended to help the CP core teaching team:

✓ analyse their strengths and areas for development

✓ leverage their strengths to upskill one another and improve the overall implementation of the CP core

✓ identify potential experts within the school who can support the team

✓ pool their resources to get as much professional development as possible through a mix of external and internal opportunities.

Example

Areas for development

Common areas that are identified for professional development by staff involved in the implementation of the CP core include:

- coaching
- mentoring
- navigating difficult conversations and topics
- alternative methods of assessment
- exploring ethics
- exploring **intercultural understanding**
- supporting reflective and reflexive practice
- using digital tools to support learning and assessment
- professional networking
- goal-setting and appraisal practices
- hosting debates
- inquiry-based education
- questioning techniques
- guiding students in their ethical use of technology.

Top tip!

It may be helpful to revisit all these questions periodically after working your way through this book. You may find that your answers change as you begin to envision how your role will look on a day-to-day basis in your specific context, and as you gain a deeper understanding of the skills required to be effective in that role.

The importance of networking

The CP framework naturally lends itself to innovation. CP schools have the autonomy and flexibility to design personalised programmes of learning that meet the aspirations and needs of their students. Much of this innovation is the result of pioneering schools and individuals creating something exciting and then sharing it with a broader network of CP schools. The schools that engage with local, regional and global networks often gain access to new CRS pathways and other opportunities.

This same entrepreneurial mindset exists at the CP core level. Many unique practices found globally within the CP core are designed in partnership between a school and one or more of its key stakeholders. The information below explores various useful networks and the importance of leveraging the power of networking to enhance the ways in which you implement the CP core.

Top tip!

Do not be afraid to reach out to any external career-related studies (CRS) providers with whom you hold agreements to leverage their expertise for professional development within your school. Many of the university and industry CRS providers are happy to include staff professional development in the collaborative agreements they sign with CP schools.

Networks to engage with

CP core staff can participate in, contribute to, and establish various networks to support the implementation of the CP core. The main ways of doing this are shown on the following page.

IB Communities

IB Communities is a network available through MyIB. One significant benefit of this network is that discussions are moderated by experienced IB practitioners.

Local/regional/global IB networks

There are local, regional and global networks dedicated to the CP core or to specific components of it. Ask the CP coordinator at your school to connect you with any available network of teachers. Alternatively, look for these kinds of groups on social media platforms, such as LinkedIn.

Job-a-Likes (JALs)

Offer to host a professional learning community, or **Job-a-Like**, for all staff in your region who perform your role. This typically involves staff responsible for a specific component of the CP core coming together for a half-day or full-day session to discuss and explore best practices. The CP coordinator can help arrange this and promote the opportunity within your local and regional IB network of schools.

IB workshop networks

Create a network with colleagues from your mandatory IB workshop. Be sure to connect with the colleagues who participate in your IB training, as they can form an excellent professional network for you going forward.

IB conference networks

Create a network with colleagues from different schools at an IB conference. This can be achieved through effective personal networking or by presenting on a topic of interest, engaging with your audience, and establishing a network of IB peers for future collaborations.

Top tip!

While local, regional and global networks can be great for collaborating and sharing with fellow educators, be aware that information on these channels is often not moderated and cannot be relied upon in the same way that IB Communities can.

Leveraging the power of networking

The group of external experts and industry leads (see Chapter 3) is unique among the stakeholder groups, because schools may not have any existing relationships with these people. This means that such relationships must be intentionally cultivated by each school or individual, and tailored to suit their specific context and students. This can be demanding, but also exciting.

This stakeholder group of external experts could be responsible for providing:

- CRS-specific mentorship programmes
- internship opportunities
- linguistic and cultural workshops
- reciprocal agreements to collaborate on community engagement
- guest speakers
- bespoke seminars in their area of expertise
- career fairs
- access to **micro-credentials**
- access to industry training.

The opportunities are limitless, framed only by school context and what is deemed desirable. External experts and industry leaders should be utilised in ways that best suit the needs of your students within the CP core. To achieve this effectively, CP core staff should be encouraged and empowered to leverage their personal and professional networks to establish enriching and impactful partnerships that benefit their students.

Example

Networking in the CP core

This example originates from a leading international school in the Asia-Pacific region that offers the DP and CP. It illustrates the significant impact that leveraging personal and professional networks can have on CP students and schools globally.

A personal and professional skills teacher reached out to the university they attended, seeking interview-preparation related workshops and career guidance for their students. The university was happy to collaborate with their alumnus and support the CP students.

After these sessions had been successfully conducted, the conversation naturally shifted to university admissions and the CRS pathways available at the school. The university was so impressed by the CP students they had worked with that they secured an agreement with the school, guaranteeing entry into the second year of some of their undergraduate degree programmes for students from specific CRS pathways, subject to grade-dependent criteria. The impact of this agreement was not only significant for the students and wider school community, but also for university recognition of the CP in that geographical location and of that particular CRS pathway.

Reflection

After exploring the section on networking, reflect on the following questions:

- Do you have any initial ideas for leveraging an existing network or professional relationship to enhance the student experience in the CP core within your school? What support might you need to make this happen, and from whom?
- Who do you know from within the school community or externally who has an extensive professional network? Can you schedule a meeting with them to discuss what you do in the CP core and identify any potential connections to their network?

Commitment to success

True professional growth extends beyond mandatory training; it is about intentionally seeking opportunities that will directly benefit your students. The CP thrives when educators collaborate, network and invest in their own development. Be bold in identifying your strengths, honest in acknowledging your areas for development, and proactive in connecting with others. Each conversation, workshop and partnership has the potential to transform the CP experience, not just for you, but for every student you work with.

Key takeaways: Chapter 4

- Personalised professional development can improve how the CP is implemented and positively impact students' learning experience.
- CP staff should reflect on their own strengths and areas for growth.
- In-school professional development can be enhanced by sharing expertise among the CP core team.
- External professional development should be strategic, resourced and linked to student impact.
- Some CRS providers may offer professional development opportunities.
- IB Communities, JALs and conferences are key platforms for CP networking.
- Leveraging networks can lead to strong partnerships and opportunities for students in the form of internships, mentorships and potentially university matriculation.

Key terms

IB Communities: moderated forums on MyIB for IB educators to connect, ask questions and share resources

Job-a-Like (JAL): a professional gathering of educators with similar roles, used to share best practices and collaborate

micro-credential: a certification that acknowledges the acquisition of specific knowledge, skills and competencies, usually achieved after a short course or programme

5 Student groupings in personal and professional skills

This chapter covers the following:

- The importance of student groupings
- Course-level decision-making on student groupings
- Classroom-level decision-making on student groupings

This chapter is intended for Career-related Programme (CP) coordinators and personal and professional skills (PPS) coordinators/teachers.

The importance of student groupings

How you decide to group students in the PPS course can influence the quality of the learning experience across the whole of the CP core. Grouping strategies can have a profound impact on student engagement and collaboration. This chapter explores the key considerations behind student grouping in PPS by offering reflective questions, real-world scenarios, and practical tips to support intentional, context-specific decision-making that aligns with your school's vision for the CP.

One of the most important decisions when it comes to the PPS component, is whether students should be grouped by their chosen career-related study (CRS). This decision exists at two levels:

- **course-level decision-making** – allocating students and staff to classes
- **classroom-level decision-making** – in-class decision-making regarding groupings for collaborative inquiries.

Course-level decision-making on student groupings

In CP cohorts that operate one PPS class, all CP students will be in the same PPS class regardless of their chosen CRS pathway. However, in larger cohorts, with multiple PPS classes, you will need to decide how to group students – by CRS or by working with students interested in a variety of career fields. There are pros and cons to each. The following example explores the decision-making process through scenarios and **probing questions** to discuss with colleagues.

Example

Scenario 1

Context: A large CP cohort with three PPS classes and eight CRS pathways represented. The CRS pathways are aeronautics, art and design, music, business, hospitality, finance, engineering, and sports business and management.

Decision to be made: Should students be grouped in PPS by CRS (as much as possible), or should students be grouped with various career-related pathways represented in each class?

Discuss the following questions:

- Could having a PPS class consisting of students from the same CRS pathway enrich the student journey, considering their shared CRS experience?
  - Might this make it easier to allocate a PPS teacher who is knowledgeable in that CRS and, therefore, potentially a better mentor to those students?
  - Would this support students in exploring concepts within the context of their chosen career field in greater depth?
- Could having a PPS class filled with students from various CRS pathways lead to more diverse and insightful collaborations, discussions and debates?
  - Could this make finding parity in student allocations and staffing more manageable, as all PPS classes will consist of various CRS pathways and a teacher who is not seen as a CRS expert in any of them?
  - Might this help students challenge the norms of their chosen career field and look at their own context through a more critical lens?
- If this scenario had the same number of PPS classes and CRS pathways, with roughly equal student numbers – making it logistically easier to achieve PPS class groupings by CRS – would this change your decision?

As always, context is key. The decisions you and your colleagues make need to reflect what is possible and what is best for your school community. The most critical part of this decision is coming to a clear understanding of why one direction would be optimal for your students. This may come down to logistics – what is possible based on student numbers, the CRS pathways selected and staff availability for PPS. However, it may depend instead on what the key decision-makers for the CP believe will give students the best experience within this component and the wider CP in your school.

Top tip!

If both options are logistically possible, consider asking a wider group of stakeholders for their input. People who may provide valuable and varied perspectives on this decision include:

- CP core staff
- CRS staff
- industry experts within the chosen CRS fields
- students
- parents.

Classroom-level decision-making on student groupings

The example below explores a scenario in which the course-level decision-making process has already been completed, and the focus is now on class-level decision-making.

Example

Scenario 2

Context: A CP cohort with two PPS classes, both consisting of 15 students split evenly among the following CRS pathways:

- hospitality
- engineering
- sports business and management.

Decision to be made: In collaborative inquiries, should students be grouped by CRS or should groups consist of students studying different CRS pathways?

Discuss the following questions:

- Do the context(s), concept(s), content or skills being explored through the inquiry matter when making this decision? If so, in what way?
- Would working with other students who have a shared understanding and similar career aspirations lead to more in-depth learning in their area of expertise?
- Is working in diverse groups more beneficial – exposing students to different perspectives, insights and ways of thinking?
- Does the approach to student groupings have to be consistent between the two classes, or can it be left to the teacher's discretion? What are the potential implications for each option?
- Do you think students will prefer CRS groupings or more diverse groupings? Why do you think that?

When deciding upon best practices within your school, remember that carefully constructed student groupings can enhance the student experience in individual inquiries and the overall PPS course. This decision should be intentional and align with your school's vision for the best way to implement the CP.

Reflection

Reflect on the following questions.

- Do you think that your key stakeholders would hold diverse beliefs on student grouping strategies?
- If so, how can you tailor the explanation and justification of your decisions on student groupings to meet your intended audience?

Top tip!

Do not be afraid to revisit your decision after each term, semester or year. Reflecting upon and then adapting practice to continually improve is an essential feature of an effective CP core implementation. Involve students as partners in gathering feedback on student groupings so that they can help affirm your choices or prompt reconsideration of practices going forward.

Commitment to success

Every grouping decision is a chance to shape how students learn from and with each other. Whether by career focus or across disciplines, your choices influence the richness of discussion, collaboration and connection in the PPS course. Be deliberate. Engage students and colleagues in the conversation. A well-considered grouping strategy doesn't just serve logistics, it sets the tone for inclusive, dynamic and transformative learning.

Key takeaways: Chapter 5

- CRS-based groupings can support depth through shared context and content.
- Mixed groupings can promote diverse thinking and collaboration.
- Context, logistics and student numbers influence these decisions, but what best supports student learning should always be the driving force.
- Consider involving a variety of stakeholders in the decision-making process.
- Review groupings regularly and adapt as necessary.

Key terms

classroom-level decision-making: decisions about how students are grouped for specific classroom tasks or collaborative projects

course-level decision-making: decisions about how students and teachers are allocated to personal and professional skills classes

probing questions: questions that are phrased in an open-ended way to encourage a detailed, informative and perhaps subjective answer

6 Crafting a classroom culture for the personal and professional skills course

This chapter covers the following:

- What a good personal and professional skills classroom culture looks like
- Effective routines for personal and professional skills
- Activities that support the creation of a high-trust classroom culture

This chapter is intended for Career-related Programme (CP) coordinators and personal and professional skills (PPS) coordinators/teachers.

What a good personal and professional skills classroom culture looks like

Due to the personalised nature of PPS, it is important to establish a **high-trust classroom culture**. This will create the conditions to best support student development and growth within this component. This kind of classroom should include the features outlined here.

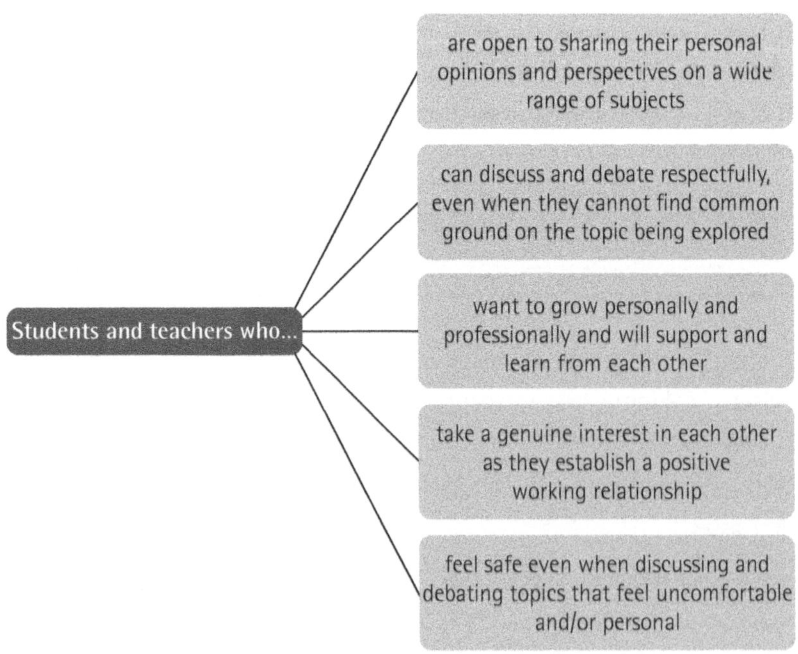

- **Students who...**
  - feel comfortable having mature peer-to-peer conversations, including giving meaningful, high-quality feedback and asking one another probing questions
  - feel comfortable enough to ask questions of themselves, each other and the teacher in pursuit of personal and professional development
  - learn as young professionals, embracing their future careers as an essential lens to frame their learning

- **Teachers who...**
  - are comfortable enough to mentor, coach and guide, taking a step back from teaching at the appropriate times to allow students to lead the learning
  - are courageous enough to contribute to challenging conversations in a way that shows their personality and perhaps vulnerabilities
  - encourage and support young people embarking upon the first stage of their professional careers

Establishing a high-trust culture requires deliberate, purposeful input from a PPS teacher and students who fully embrace the philosophy. This chapter explores strategies that you can use to establish a high-trust culture in your classroom, facilitating the best environment possible for student development and growth.

Effective routines for personal and professional skills

One feature of a high-trust classroom culture is a series of routines associated with specific moments. Some examples of these are outlined below.

As students enter the classroom

One of the best things you can do is to show students that you care about them, both as students and as individuals. A quick way to do this is to meet each student as they enter the class and ask them how they are doing. Follow up by asking them how they are getting on with an extracurricular activity that they are passionate about, or how their career-related studies classes are progressing. This may sound obvious, but interactions like this can have a big impact on students, and they can influence how students engage in their PPS course.

As these routines become part of classroom life, take time to share with students *why* you value them. Explain that you want to know more about their lives because genuine interest builds trust and rapport. Then encourage them to try this kind of interaction themselves – with you, their classmates and other teachers in the school when greeting them. In a later lesson, ask students for their reflections. Did it help them build rapport with others? Could they recognise any positive personal or professional by-products of this practice?

Taking an active interest

As a follow-up to the first routine, you could use the first five minutes of class as a semi-structured conversation time, during which students can catch up about their learning in career-related studies classes or get to know one another a little better. You can also pop in and out of conversations to get to know your students and ensure time is used meaningfully.

You could create a list of accepted conversation topics with students to facilitate this routine, such as:

- previous learning in PPS
- progress with their career-related studies, components of the CP core or Diploma Programme classes
- interesting news from a student's chosen career field
- any recent participation in extracurricular activities or representing the school
- any important news stories that are current or relevant to them.

Sharing context

Throughout the PPS course, you may decide to use student presentations as planned activities in inquiries or even as **formative assessments** or **summative assessments** (see Chapter 8). To contextualise the activity or assessment for a student and their chosen career, ask them to share a few key pieces of information at the start of every presentation, including:

- their name
- their career-related studies pathway
- what skill(s) they were trying to develop within this inquiry
- which specific area/topic they are hoping to get feedback on.

This will refresh students' memories so they know who the presenter is, why they are a CP student, and what they aim to achieve through their chosen CRS pathway. This will ensure that feedback is focused on the presenter's context. It will also help students build stronger connections and rapport as they share their aspirations and reasons with one another. This consistent sharing develops a high-trust classroom culture.

Debating and challenging conversations

The PPS course can lead to challenging conversations, especially as students explore ethical dilemmas, cultural differences and other controversial topics. It is important to prepare for this by ensuring that students know how to discuss and debate serious and potentially divisive issues.

You should establish a routine for conducting debates and potentially challenging conversations within the class. Ideally, students would contribute to the creation of these routines and help to establish useful protocols to ensure that these experiences are enriching and impactful. When you have decided on the routines and protocols, you could create a poster for the classroom wall for students to refer to in these situations. An example is shown below. Note that there could be many different routines and protocols, so ensure that the ones you include are suitable for and agreed upon by your student cohort.

Routines and protocols for debates and challenging conversations

- Only one person speaks at a time, with a time limit set for each contribution before the conversation/debate begins. The time limit will vary depending on the number of participants and the nature of the debate or conversation.
- When questioning or preparing a response, focus only on the ideas or perspectives shared, not on the person who shared them.
- Use questions such as 'What makes you think that way?' *after* the debate or conversation – and within the personal and professional studies class – to stimulate reflection and growth. Always think about your tone and the way you ask this question to ensure that it is perceived as a reflective prompt, not a negative comment about someone's opinion.
- Do not continue the debates outside the classroom. If more time is required, it will be made available during the next PPS class so that it can continue to be carried out in a controlled environment.
- Never forget that the purpose of these conversations and debates is to improve understanding and learn from the varied and valued perspectives within the class.
- Always remember that you do not need to agree with someone on every issue to maintain an effective working relationship. It is possible to respect and trust someone who has different opinions from you.

Top tip!

To aid students in focusing on the idea/perspective rather than the individual who presents it, you could assign them a viewpoint to represent that differs from their own opinion.

Example

The trolley problem

When you feel the class is ready to test an established debate routine, introduce the ethical dilemma of the **trolley problem**. This will almost certainly lead to differences in opinion and is a great starting point for a discussion on ethical thinking.

As the discussion develops, offer ideas to make the dilemma more challenging – for example, you could change the scenario to different contexts or introduce the idea that friends and family are involved. Doing so can prompt an exploration of which elements of culture and personal experiences can contribute to an individual's ethical and moral thinking. This type of activity can help prepare students for the reflective project, develop their ability to examine various perspectives, and understand how bias is formed in themselves and others.

Getting involved in the trolley problem debate is a good opportunity to model the desired behaviour and build rapport with your students, helping to establish a high-trust culture. When constructed carefully, a debate can be a fantastic tool to increase understanding and appreciation of multiple perspectives on an issue.

Activities that support the creation of a high-trust classroom culture

Activities created with the main purpose of establishing a high-trust classroom culture can also bring other benefits. Some examples are given below.

Planning time with students

The best possible version of PPS is one that includes meaningful student input. In fact, you are expected to co-create inquiries with students. You can set aside collaborative planning time with students, which could include:

- an explanation of the nature of PPS, including the framework of the course, learning outcomes, and the relationship between concepts, contexts, content and skills
- an explanation that your role is to teach, guide, mentor, coach and support students in connecting learning across their academic programme as they develop desirable and valuable personal and professional skills that can be applied in a variety of contexts
- an opportunity for students to contribute their ideas individually and collectively, suggesting areas of interest for inquiry throughout their PPS experience, considering their strengths, areas for development and aspirations
- an opportunity for you to share some of your planned inquiries and receive feedback from your students.

This kind of discussion could occur at several points in the PPS journey. If possible, meet with students for planning time before the first year of the CP (CP 1) begins. This gives you the most time to act on student feedback and suggestions before the course starts. Alternatively, you could allocate time at the beginning of the PPS course in CP 1, then incorporate student feedback as early as possible, exploring suggestions for future inquiries in the following terms/semesters. You could repeat this process throughout the PPS journey to inform planning for future terms/semesters/CP 2.

Seeking feedback from students improves the quality of the personal and professional studies course by making it more personalised and relevant for students. It also makes students partners in the planning process, which supports the creation of positive working relationships and lays the foundations for a high-trust culture within the class. This activity is also incredibly useful when preparing to incorporate **student-led inquiries** into the PPS curriculum.

Top tip!

Consider repeating this process with the parents of CP students, to include them as partners and lean on their knowledge to help personalise the learning for each student and cohort. If you think this would be useful within your context, be sure to let your students know in advance, so they know why their parents are being invited to school.

Designing the classroom

Creating the optimal physical environment in the classroom helps to set the right tone and ensure students are comfortable. Imagine hosting an intense ethical debate with students sitting in a traditional classroom with single desks equally spaced, all facing in the same direction; it would not produce the required atmosphere for open debate and discussion. A more inviting setup might include soft seating spaces positioned so that students can make eye contact and address each other more easily.

You can involve students in planning the classroom layout to ensure that it functions well for their needs in the PPS context. To facilitate this activity, you could:

- make time before CP 1 or at the beginning of the PPS course
- explain the kinds of activities that PPS consists of so students know what functions the classroom environment needs to support
- allow time for students to compile ideas, and support them with any funding requests that may come from their suggestions (if appropriate and useful)
- compile examples of what the classroom layout could be, depending on the resources available at your school – then ask students to choose (this removes the need for any funding conversations).

A well-designed physical environment helps create the right atmosphere for diverse PPS inquiries and learning.

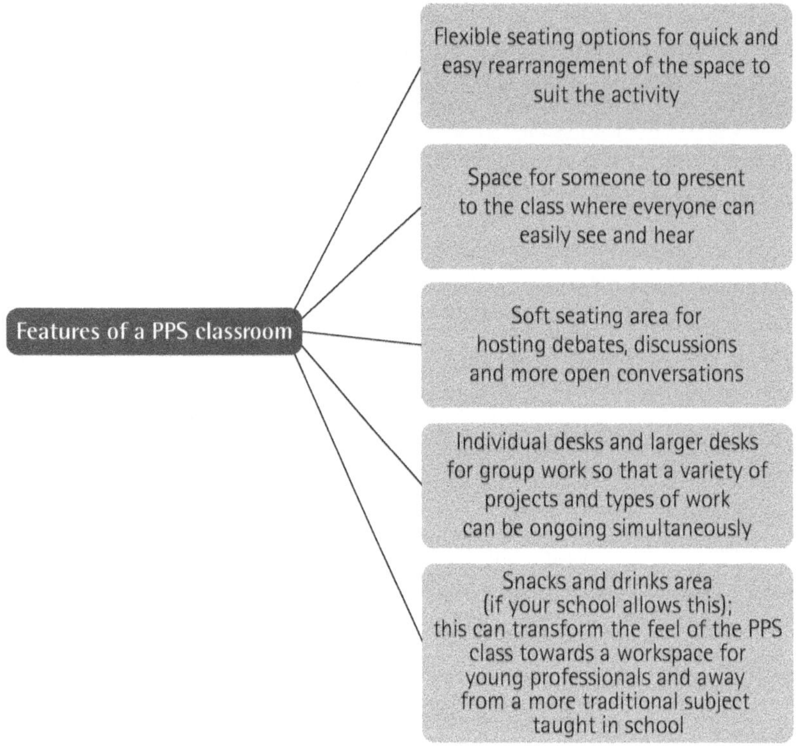

Time for adaptation

Expect the unexpected and set aside time to allow it to happen. You should be aware of the need to adapt and allow for spontaneous inquiries, debates or activities that arise. Some of the best, most impactful learning in PPS can happen in unexpected moments. Capitalising on these opportunities and allowing them to flourish can create some of the most rewarding moments within a PPS classroom. Planning this time as an activity every so often – particularly when it is anticipated that a particular topic might prompt extraneous conversation or debate – gives you the flexibility and autonomy to explore areas of particular interest in more depth or devote more time to continuing exciting conversations as and when they come up.

Teachers are often focused on covering all required content before final assessments. In contrast, the nature of PPS allows space for 'eureka' moments, giving classes time to explore the growth such discoveries can bring. If this time is built into planning but not needed, it can instead be used for student-led inquiries or collaborative planning of future projects.

Celebrating and sharing success

Reflective and reflexive practice play a huge role in the PPS course and across the CP core. In the context of PPS, the IB defines reflection and reflexivity in the following way:

'An intentional, active and ongoing process of reviewing one's thinking, practice and actions, examining views and assumptions, and being open to having one's own perspectives challenged and changed. It takes on a variety of forms: metacognitive and process reflection, critical reflection, self-reflexivity and critical reflexivity.' (Personal and Professional Skills Guide, IBO, 2025)

Reflection is a normal part of learning and is included as a specific step in the PPS inquiry cycle. Creating a specific activity for students to reflect on their recent personal and professional experiences, then identifying and celebrating successes, is an excellent way of encouraging reflective and reflexive practices while contributing to a positive classroom culture. This activity can be incorporated as a short segment of a specific inquiry or as a separate activity every few months, depending on what works best in the context of each class. The positive outcomes of this activity are as follows:

Students	Teachers
• get a confidence boost as they share their successes and are celebrated among their peers • understand what each of their classmates values in themselves through their choice of what to share, contributing to the creation of a high-trust classroom culture.	• have an opportunity to prompt students to reflect on their successes and recognise the effective practices that led to those outcomes • can encourage students to consider why they chose those specific successes to share, helping them clarify their goals, values, and personal definitions of achievement; this supports both reflective and reflexive thinking.

Examples

Scenario 1

Reflections

During a short sharing session at the beginning of a learning engagement, a student shares that they have recently started attending a running club three times a week and they are noticing a positive impact on their physical, mental and social wellbeing. Through attending the running club, the student feels they are achieving a better balance in life and have noticed improvements to their physical health alongside a reduction in stress levels. They are also enjoying developing new friendships outside their current personal and professional networks.

Outcomes

Through processing some questions asked by the teacher, the student noted that they have discovered the importance of having friends outside of their workplace (in this case, school) as it helps them find a better balance between their personal and professional lives.

Scenario 2

Reflections

During a scheduled discussion session, a student shares that they recently received excellent feedback on a performance from one of their Berklee College of Music professors as part of their career-related study in music. This gave them the confidence to ask the professor for a letter of recommendation, which they kindly agreed to provide. The student is immensely proud of their performance and the recognition they have received, and they are delighted to add a letter of recommendation from an esteemed member of the Berklee College of Music faculty to their university applications.

Outcomes

Through a discussion with a friend in the class, the student realised that they would not have asked for the letter of recommendation if they had not received the excellent feedback, due to a lack of self-confidence and intrinsic belief in their ability. As a result, the student will focus their next student-led inquiry on developing self-confidence for the workplace.

Top tip!

Get involved and share your success as well! This is another opportunity to model desired behaviour and build rapport with your students. It is especially powerful if you explain the personal or professional goals behind the success that you shared. This will position you as a role model for continued personal and professional development, setting a great example for your students.

The CP thrives in many countries, cultures and contexts. Most – if not all – of the shared strategies to support personal and professional skills teachers in building high-trust cultures are universally applicable, but some will work better than others, depending on the context.

Reflection

Considering the goal is to create a high-trust culture within your PPS classroom(s), explore the following reflection questions with your CP core team:

- How well do you know the students that you work with?
- Do you know why your CP students chose this programme and their career-related studies?
- Do you know their aspirations and motivations?
- Do you know what they value when building trust with another person or within a group of people? What do they see as trustworthy?
- Do any of the shared routines or activities resonate with your approach to implementing the CP core?
- Are any of the shared routines or activities not suitable for your context? If so, why?
- What other strategies would you employ to build a high-trust culture and create the optimal PPS environment in your context?
- For schools with multiple PPS classes and teachers, would you mandate the use of any routines or activities across your PPS classes, or should these be implemented at the teacher's discretion?
- Has this section changed your idea of what it means to be an effective PPS teacher? If so, in what way?

Commitment to success

A high-trust classroom culture does not happen by chance; it is built moment by moment, through intentional choices. From the seating plan to the way you greet students, everything contributes to the culture you shape. As a PPS educator, you set the tone. Use that influence wisely. Design your environment with care, co-create routines with students, and model openness and empathy. When students feel safe and seen, transformative learning follows!

Key takeaways: Chapter 6

- A high-trust classroom culture is essential in PPS and must be intentionally built through consistent teacher actions.
- Effective routines, such as personal greetings and context sharing, can help establish rapport among teachers and students.
- Activities such as collaborative planning, classroom design and celebrating successes can deepen student engagement and agency.
- There is a shared responsibility between teachers and students to craft a safe, engaging and personalised PPS learning environment.

Key terms

formative assessment: ongoing evaluation during inquiries that guides student learning and development

high-trust classroom culture: a learning environment where students and teachers feel safe, respected, and open to sharing, learning and challenging ideas together

student-led inquiry: an inquiry planned and directed by the student, encouraging autonomy and personal relevance

summative assessment: formal evaluation at the end of an inquiry to measure achievement of learning outcomes

trolley problem: a philosophical ethical dilemma where participants must choose between allowing a runaway trolley to run its course, injuring five people, or actively changing its path so that it only injures one person instead. This is used to introduce ethical thinking and stimulate discussion on bias, values and ethical decision-making

7 Planning your personal and professional skills curriculum

This chapter covers the following:

- An overview of the personal and professional skills course requirements
- Constructing an inquiry
- A sample curriculum map for personal and professional skills
- Collaborative planning in the personal and professional skills course

This chapter is intended for Career-related Programme (CP) coordinators and personal and professional skills (PPS) coordinators/teachers.

An overview of the personal and professional skills course requirements

The IB's personal and professional skills guide states the following requirements.

- A minimum of 100 guided learning hours over two years
- A focus on at least four concepts from the personal and professional skills framework:
  - Change
  - Connections
  - Identities
  - Perspectives
  - Systems
  - Wellbeing
- A minimum of eight skills developed across four domains:
  - At least two skills from the **intrapersonal skills** domain.
  - At least two skills from the **interpersonal skills** domain.
  - At least two skills from the thinking skills domain.
  - At least two skills from the intercultural understanding skills domain.
- Each skill must be developed in at least two of the eight contexts:
  - Career-related studies
  - Community engagement
  - Diploma Programme courses
  - Informal learning
  - Language and cultural studies
  - Personal life

  - Professional life
  - Reflective project
- Evidence of progress against each of the five learning outcomes:
  - LO1: Develop and apply intrapersonal skills in various contexts.
  - LO2: Develop and apply communication and interpersonal skills in various contexts.
  - LO3: Develop and apply thinking skills in a variety of contexts.
  - LO4: Develop and apply intercultural understanding in a variety of contexts.
  - LO5: Demonstrate an awareness of the ethical implications of one's choices and actions on self and others.
- A student-curated portfolio that shows learning and growth over the two-year PPS journey, demonstrates the stated requirements, and provides opportunity for student reflection.

A carefully constructed **curriculum map** will meet all these requirements through teacher-led, collaboratively planned and student-led inquiries across the two-year course.

Constructing an inquiry

Inquiry lies at the heart of IB educational philosophy. From the early years through to graduation, this approach fosters curiosity, critical thinking and meaningful engagement. By involving students in questioning, research, investigation, collaboration and reflection, inquiry connects them to their work on a deeper level. This active process encourages students to take ownership of their learning, promotes lifelong learning habits and equips them with the skills to navigate an ever-changing world. The PPS course is anchored in inquiry-based learning, offering students opportunities to explore real-world issues, develop **transversal skills** that they can apply in a wide variety of situations, and reflect on their personal and professional growth.

A sample curriculum map for personal and professional skills

The sample curriculum map that follows shows an example of a two-year overview for a 100-hour PPS course. It demonstrates how a single inquiry can be constructed within the PPS framework and how it could be part of a larger series of inquiries that work together to meet the IB requirements. Note that each inquiry is made up of a series of learning experiences to allow ongoing inquiry and reflection throughout. This example also includes scheduled time for a student-led inquiry, allowing students to investigate an area of their choosing to ensure that the curriculum is relevant and purposeful to them and their unique context. Additionally, student-led inquiries could make up a regular part of each larger series of inquiries focusing on one topic. (Note that the inquiries in this example 100-hour course, can be accessed in full in Chapter 9.)

This curriculum map can be used as an example of how to structure the PPS course to deliver students an engaging and meaningful experience while meeting the IB's requirements for this component.

Inquiry title	Focus question	Concepts covered	Contexts applied	Skills developed	Learning outcomes addressed	Timeframe
Knowing Ourselves, Connecting with Others	How can understanding ourselves help us connect with others and contribute to a global community?	Identities Connections Perspectives	Personal Life Career-related study Language and cultural studies	Self-awareness Collaboration and networking Communication Critical thinking	LO1, LO2, LO4	Year 1 10 hours 5 learning engagements
Applied ethics: Inquiry into the application of key ethical theories in the personal and professional world	How can different ethical theories guide decision-making in personal and professional contexts, and what are the strengths and limitations of each?	Perspectives Identities	Career-related studies Reflective project Personal life Professional life Language and cultural studies	Self-awareness Ethical decision-making Reflection and reflexivity	LO3, LO5	Year 1 20 hours 8 learning engagements
Adapting to change: Thriving in a rapidly evolving world	How can individuals and organisations adapt to change while maintaining wellbeing and ethical integrity?	Change Connections Wellbeing Perspectives	Professional life Personal life Informal learning Community engagement	Adaptability Resilience Communication Problem-solving	LO1, LO2, LO3, LO5	Year 1 20 hours 9 learning engagements
Ethical decision-making in the digital age	How can individuals and organisations make ethical decisions in digital spaces when using AI, social media and personal data?	Systems Perspectives	Career-related study Reflective project Professional life	Ethical decision-making Critical thinking Communication Information literacy	LO2, LO3, LO5	Year 1 20 hours 7 learning engagements

Inquiry title	Focus question	Concepts covered	Contexts applied	Skills developed	Learning outcomes addressed	Timeframe
Cultural identity in a globalised workplace	How do cultural backgrounds influence professional identity and shape interactions in a globalised workplace?	Identities Connections Perspectives	Language and cultural studies Professional life Community engagement	Empathy Social awareness Collaboration and networking Communication	LO2, LO4	Year 2 15 hours 7 learning engagements
The psychology of leadership and influence	How do different leadership styles and persuasion techniques affect others, and what ethical considerations should guide their use?	Systems Change Perspectives	Professional life Community engagement Informal learning	Leadership Change management and conflict mediation Ethical decision-making Self-management	LO1, LO2, LO5	Year 2 15 hours 7 learning engagements
Student-led inquiry (open topic)	Students design their own inquiry based on interests and career aspirations	Varies based on student selection	Determined by student	Determined by student	Determined by student	Year 2 10 hours

This two-year curriculum map meets the following requirements:

- ✓ Exploration of at least four concepts.
- ✓ Development of at least two intrapersonal skills explored in at least two contexts.
- ✓ Development of at least two interpersonal skills explored in at least two contexts.
- ✓ Development of at least two thinking skills explored in at least two contexts.
- ✓ Development of at least two intercultural understanding skills explored in at least two contexts.
- ✓ Opportunity for development and growth against the five learning outcomes.

Components of an inquiry

Each inquiry in the PPS course should include several key components to ensure it aligns with IB expectations and provides a meaningful learning experience. Consider the example below:

Inquiry title	Focus area	Focus question	Concepts covered	Contexts applied	Skills developed	Learning outcomes addressed
Adapting to change: Thriving in a rapidly evolving world	Exploring how individuals and organisations respond to change, developing adaptability and resilience	How can individuals and organisations adapt to change while maintaining wellbeing and ethical integrity?	Change Connections Wellbeing Perspectives	Professional life Personal life Informal learning Community engagement	Adaptability Resilience Communication Problem-solving	LO1, LO2, LO3, LO5

Inquiry title

The title of an inquiry should be concise and engaging, hinting at the concepts and skills that will be explored. It should spark curiosity in students and provide a clear direction for the inquiry.

Example

'Adapting to change: Thriving in a rapidly evolving world'

This title immediately signals that the inquiry will deal with change – a PPS concept – and suggests that students will explore how to adapt and thrive in shifting personal or professional landscapes.

Top tip!

Note that the inquiry title is not an IB requirement – it is only part of the portfolio, not part of the lesson planning.

Focus question

The focus question should give a key focus to the inquiry. It should be both engaging and challenging, and something that is referred to throughout and at the end of the inquiry.

Example

'How can individuals and organisations adapt to change while maintaining wellbeing and ethical integrity?'

This focus question makes it clear that students will examine the nature of change in the contexts of both personal and professional life contexts. They will explore how individuals and organisations respond to rapid shifts – whether technological, social or environmental – and reflect on their own adaptability. Students will investigate real-world examples of change management and consider how to develop resilience and adaptability in their own lives and future careers.

Concepts covered

The PPS framework identifies six concepts around which all inquiries should be built.

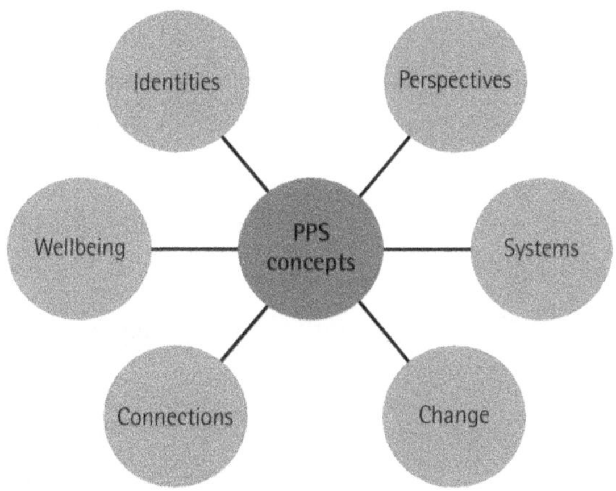

A minimum of four concepts must be addressed over the two-year course, although more can be incorporated into the design of any inquiry. Teachers can decide whether to focus on one concept or several. The decision may be informed by the design of the whole two-year curriculum, and may also vary depending on students' needs and school context.

Example

Main context

Change: Understanding how individuals and organisations evolve and adapt to shifting circumstances.

Possible additional concepts

Connections: Exploring the relationships between personal growth, professional development and societal trends.

Wellbeing: Considering the impact of change on mental, emotional and physical health.

Perspectives: Analysing how different people and cultures perceive and respond to change.

Contexts applied

Each inquiry could be applied in multiple contexts to encourage the transferability of skills. The number of contexts explored will depend on several factors, including the school's local and global context, the current CP cohort, and the two-year PPS curriculum plan. For example, a large CP cohort with multiple PPS classes might explore the same inquiry through distinct professional contexts – such as ethics in business, design and medicine – across different classes, highlighting interdisciplinary connections. Conversely, a small cohort with one PPS class of three or four students may take a more integrated approach, tailoring the inquiry to each student's Career-related Study. A single inquiry on **ethical decision-making**, for instance, could simultaneously explore sports, digital media and sustainability, fostering personalised yet collaborative learning. This may result in schools approaching similar inquiries, yet addressing different concepts, skills and even learning outcomes.

Example

For the inquiry 'Adapting to change: Thriving in a rapidly evolving world', by applying the concept of change in varied contexts, students will gain a holistic understanding of how adaptable skills can be used across life domains.

Professional life: Investigating how businesses and organisations manage change (for example, adopting new technologies or restructuring teams).

Personal life: Reflecting on personal experiences with change, such as transitioning to a new environment or overcoming challenges.

Informal learning: Exploring how change is navigated in extracurricular activities, sports or social groups.

Reflective project: Discussions around ethical decision-making in the face of change within multiple career fields, which can help teachers and students relate to ethical dilemmas and prepare for the reflective project.

Skills developed

Inquiries should focus on developing transversal skills from the four domains:

- intrapersonal skills
- interpersonal skills
- thinking skills
- intercultural understanding.

Intrapersonal skills
- Adaptability
- Reflection and reflexivity
- Resilience
- Self-advocacy
- Self-awareness
- Self-management

Interpersonal skills
- Change management and conflict mediation
- Collaboration and networking
- Communication
- Leadership

Thinking skills
- Critical thinking
- Creative thinking
- Ethical decision-making
- Information literacy
- Problem-solving
- Reflection and reflexivity
- Systems thinking

Intercultural understanding
- Change management and conflict mediation
- Civic and social responsibility
- Empathy
- Ethics and personal values
- Reflection and reflexivity
- Self-efficacy
- Social awareness

Students must develop at least two skills from each domain throughout the course. Each skill must be applied in at least two contexts.

Example

The 'Adapting to change: Thriving in a rapidly evolving world' inquiry example chooses to focus on the following skills, to ensure that students understand change intellectually and develop the tools to navigate it effectively in their own lives.

Intrapersonal skills	Interpersonal skills	Thinking skills
Adaptability: Learning to adjust to new situations and environments. **Resilience:** Building the ability to recover from setbacks and persevere through challenges.	**Communication:** Communication involves sharing meaning through various forms – not just words but also gestures, body language and visuals.	**Problem-solving:** Identifying and implementing solutions to challenges brought by change.

Learning outcomes addressed

Each inquiry should focus on at least one of the five PPS learning outcomes:

- LO1: Develop and apply intrapersonal skills in a variety of contexts.
- LO2: Develop and apply communication and interpersonal skills in a variety of contexts.
- LO3: Develop and apply thinking skills in a variety of contexts.
- LO4: Develop and apply intercultural understanding in a variety of contexts.
- LO5: Demonstrate an awareness of the ethical implications of one's choices and actions on self and others.

While a single inquiry may not address all five, the curriculum must ensure that students demonstrate growth in all outcomes over the two-year course.

Example

The 'Adapting to change: Thriving in a rapidly evolving world' inquiry offers rich opportunities to address multiple learning outcomes, ensuring a comprehensive learning experience:

LO1: Students will reflect on their own adaptability and resilience, setting personal goals for growth.

LO3: Students will analyse case studies of change management and develop problem-solving strategies.

LO5: Students will consider the ethical dimensions of change, including how decisions affect individuals and communities.

Top tip!

Remember – for any given inquiry, it may be more appropriate to focus on just one or two learning outcomes. Once again, this depends on the needs of your school and student cohort. It is up to the educators and planning team to determine the best model.

Opportunities for reflection and portfolio evidence

Reflection is a core component of the PPS course, so each inquiry should include opportunities for students to reflect on their learning and document their progress in their PPS portfolio.

Example

Here are some examples of reflection and portfolio evidence for the 'Adapting to change: Thriving in a rapidly evolving world' inquiry.

Personal reflection journal: Students could keep a journal documenting how their understanding of change evolves throughout the inquiry.

Case study analysis: Students could analyse a real-world example of change (for example, a company undergoing digital transformation) and reflect on the strategies used.

Ethical dilemma response: Students could write a reflective piece exploring an ethical dilemma related to change, considering the perspectives of different stakeholders.

These portfolio artefacts would provide tangible evidence of skill development and progress towards the learning outcomes.

Structuring an inquiry

Inquiries in the PPS course follow a flexible, cyclical process designed to promote deep learning and critical reflection. This is split into five stages, as shown in the graphic below.

Inquiries vary in both nature and in the way they are organised, so they do not always need to follow these stages in order.

Top tip!

The reflection might sometimes come after the sharing stage, as it can be valuable for students to be able to reflect on their sharing experience.

Example

For the 'Adapting to change: Thriving in a rapidly evolving world' inquiry:

Focus

The focus question for the example is:

'How can individuals and organisations adapt to change while maintaining their wellbeing and ethical integrity?'

This invites students to think broadly about the nature of change and to consider both personal and professional dimensions.

Explore

Students might:

- research change management theories and models
- analyse case studies of organisations that successfully navigated change
- conduct interviews with professionals who have experienced significant career changes
- reflect on personal experiences with change.

Act

Students might:

- design and implement a personal change plan (for example, setting and achieving a personal goal)
- participate in a group project that requires adapting to unexpected challenges (this could be linked to a community engagement project)
- create a presentation on ethical considerations in change management.

Reflect

Students might ask themselves:

- How has my understanding of change evolved throughout this inquiry?
- What strategies have I developed for managing change in my own life?
- How do ethical considerations influence the way individuals and organisations respond to change?

Share

Students might:

- present their findings from case study analyses to the class, other PPS classes or other peers, such as theory of knowledge classes, grade/year-level advisory classes, or at a school-wide assembly
- share personal reflections in a class discussion or online forum
- submit portfolio artefacts for peer review and feedback.

In addition to teacher-directed inquiries, student-led and collaboratively planned inquiries offer valuable opportunities for students to take ownership of their learning. The teacher acts as a mentor and guide, helping students design the inquiry, select the concepts and skills to explore and determine the final output. Whether fully student-created or co-created with the teacher, these inquiries encourage creativity, problem-solving and independence, providing students with a deeper sense of agency and investment in their learning.

Collaborative planning in the personal and professional skills course

Collaborative planning refers to PPS teachers working alongside:

- the CP core team
- DP teachers
- CRS teachers/providers
- other key stakeholders
- pastoral/wellbeing leads within the school
- students
- parents
- CP alumni.

It is important to work closely with the rest of the CP core team so that each component can leverage the learning across the core to support student engagement and growth within its own component. This allows staff to plan for specific activities within their respective components that make the most of learning across the whole core. It also allows connections to be made explicit across the core and intentional scaffolding of critical thinking across the four components, while avoiding overlaps.

Top tip!

Do not underestimate input from CP alumni. These stakeholders are uniquely positioned to give feedback, based on their experience and understanding of all aspects of the CP and CP core in your school context. Inviting CP alumni into the PPS planning process allows you to hear what was most impactful and what students felt was missing from the course that would have made them feel better-prepared. This perspective is incredibly valuable in fine-tuning the curriculum map and individual inquiries from cohort to cohort.

Commitment to success

A thoughtfully planned and collaboratively designed curriculum map is the foundation of a successful PPS course. By mapping out your two-year journey in advance – while still allowing space for adaptation – you ensure that every student receives a coherent and impactful experience that meets IB expectations and responds to their unique contexts and aspirations. Your commitment to intentional, student-centred planning will ensure that the PPS course is not just compliant – it is transformative.

Key takeaways: Chapter 7

- A curriculum map can ensure your PPS course meets IB requirements and delivers a coherent student experience.
- Commit to inquiry as your planning lens. Let real-world relevance and student curiosity drive the design of each unit.
- Inquiries follow a cyclical, although not necessarily linear, process:
  Focus → Explore → Act → Reflect → Share.
- Review and revise regularly – use feedback from students, teachers and alumni to adapt inquiries and better meet the evolving needs of each cohort.
- Build in reflection from the start. Ensure students have regular opportunities to reflect, document progress, and curate portfolio artefacts throughout their learning.
- Collaborative planning with key stakeholders can enhance the quality of inquiries and curriculum alignment.
- Use the examples provided to spark your own curiosity and creative processes as you consider which inquiries you will create for your students.

Key terms

curriculum map: a structured plan showing how the personal and professional skills course will meet all IB requirements

ethical decision-making: the process of choosing a course of action when faced with moral questions or dilemmas; this involves evaluating different options based on your ethical values and considering the consequences for all people affected, to arrive at a responsible and justifiable choice

interpersonal skills: the behaviours people use to interact successfully with other people, such as communication, collaboration and teamwork

intrapersonal skills: the strategies people use to understand their own behaviour and emotions, to become more self-aware

transversal skills: skills that can be used in a wide variety of situations and settings, rather than being specific to a job or academic discipline

8 Assessment in personal and professional skills

This chapter covers the following:

- Good practice in assessment
- When and how to assess
- Deciding on a grading scale
- Giving feedback
- Determining portfolio completion
- Reporting to parents

This chapter is intended for Career-related Programme (CP) coordinators and personal and professional skills (PPS) coordinators/teachers.

Good practice in assessment

Assessment is vital in supporting and measuring skill development in the PPS course. PPS teachers should ensure that both formative assessments and summative assessments align with the learning outcomes and promote student growth across the inquiry-based learning model.

Assessment in PPS should be purposeful and aligned with the inquiry-based approach. In this context, formative and summative assessments serve different purposes, and understanding when and how to use each type will ensure a meaningful evaluation of student progress.

Formative assessments

- This type of assessment is ongoing and takes place throughout the inquiries.
- The aim of formative assessment here is to track skill development and provide immediate feedback to guide students in their learning process.
- These assessments can take many forms, from quick peer reviews to reflective journals, and allow students to adjust before they are evaluated more formally.

Summative assessments

- These assessments measure student progress after an inquiry.
- They evaluate whether students have met the defined learning outcomes and clearly indicate their progress.
- Summative assessments should align with the reporting timelines of your school to ensure that grades reflect accurate reporting of progress towards the learning outcomes, and allow you to communicate this progress with students and families.

When and how to assess

The nature of PPS assessment is ongoing and continuous – a hallmark of good practice in inquiry-based learning. You should focus on providing consistent opportunities for feedback and reflection, which are essential for skill development. These assessments should align with the school's reporting timelines, allowing you to accurately report on student progress and provide feedback that will guide continued growth.

Formative assessments

Formative assessments can take many forms throughout an inquiry. Examples include:

- peer feedback on project work or presentations
- self-reflection journals, where students track their growth in PPS
- exit tickets or short responses at the end of a lesson to gauge understanding of concepts
- in-class discussions or group work where students demonstrate their ability to collaborate and communicate
- quizzes or knowledge checks after key parts of an inquiry to assess how well students have retained concepts.

Summative assessments

In contrast, summative assessments are usually conducted at the end of each inquiry, to evaluate how well students have achieved the learning outcomes associated with the inquiry.

Summative assessments are more formal and may include:

- presentations (individual or group) on the inquiry topic
- written reports or reflections that summarise the inquiry process and its findings
- multimedia projects such as videos or podcasts that showcase the application of skills and concepts learned throughout the inquiry.

The flexibility of the PPS course means that it is possible to assess students in ways that you cannot do in other subjects. It also offers an opportunity to mirror real-world challenges and the four formats in which students might present their reflective project: written, audio, visual and audio-visual. These assessments can be engaging and help students develop the skills they will need in further education and their careers.

Top tip!

Consider mixing traditional assessments with innovative approaches.

Presentations: Allow students to present their findings or reflections, practising public speaking and presentation skills.

Debates: Use debates to assess critical thinking and communication skills in a professional setting.

Mock interviews: Simulate job interviews, in which students apply their communication and problem-solving skills.

Podcasts or videos: Encourage students to create multimedia projects where they reflect on their inquiry, providing an alternative to written assessments.

Deciding on a grading scale

The **grading scale** for PPS should align with your school's assessment policy while also reflecting the flexibility provided by the IB in how assessments are conducted. The key is to ensure that the grading scale is meaningful and consistent with other subjects, while accurately assessing the learning outcomes of the PPS course.

Many schools choose to align their PPS grading scale with Diploma Programme subjects using the 1–7 scale, or with the reflective project using an A–E scale. Schools with a singular career-related study may choose to align their PPS grading scale with that of their CRS. This ensures consistency, familiarity of terminology and coherence with the broader school assessment system.

Top tip!

When considering assessment and grading scales in PPS, talk to the university and college counselling team and other relevant stakeholders in the academic team. They may offer a valuable perspective when it comes to transcripts and university applications.

Giving feedback

Feedback is essential for student growth and skills development. It should be timely, specific and aligned with school policy. The goal of feedback in PPS is to help students refine their skills.

Feedback should be...

Timely

Feedback should be provided regularly throughout an inquiry, especially for formative assessments. This gives students the opportunity to reflect on feedback and make improvements before summative assessments. For example, if students are developing a presentation, feedback during the preparation stage will help improve the final presentation.

Specific and actionable

Feedback should be clear and constructive. Rather than vague comments like 'Good job', explain *why* something works and *how* students can improve. For example: 'Your communication is clear, but you could provide more real-world examples to make your argument more relatable.'

In a variety of formats

Feedback can be provided in many formats such as:

- written comments on assignments, reflections or projects
- oral feedback during one-on-one check-ins or after presentations
- peer feedback during group activities or collaborative projects
- rubrics that clearly define expectations and performance levels.

Aligned with school policy

The format and timing of feedback should align with your school's feedback policy, ensuring consistency across subjects. Regardless of the format, feedback should always encourage reflection and highlight specific steps for improvement.

Determining portfolio completion

Deciding what constitutes successful completion of the PPS course is a school-based decision. The requirements outlined in Chapter 7 and in the IB documentation should be met, of course, but what that ultimately looks like will vary between schools and cohort years. However, it is essential to develop clear criteria, to ensure that teachers, students and parents all understand what successful completion of this component involves. It is also important to support teachers in contextualising and structuring their feedback on potential curated artefacts for their students' portfolios.

When considering what might comprise successful course completion and portfolio guidance in your school, explore the following questions within the PPS teaching team to help develop a shared understanding of best practice.

- Can the portfolio be digital or analogue?
- If it will be digital, will a particular application be prescribed, or can students choose how to compile their portfolio?
- Will students be able to use various media types when curating their portfolio?
- Will you create and explore example artefacts with students to model what an artefact can look like?
- Will you set a minimum/maximum number of artefacts students can use in their portfolio? Does this allow students to showcase their learning and evidence the minimum requirements regarding concepts, contexts, skills and learning outcomes?
- Will you establish checkpoints where, according to the PPS curriculum map, students should have a certain number of curated artefacts showing evidence of growth against a set number of concepts, contexts, skills and learning outcomes?
- How will students and teachers ensure the minimum requirements have been evidenced through the portfolio?
- Will there be guiding questions to support student reflection on each artefact and the portfolio in its entirety?

Top tip!

Use the same feedback process for adapting inquiries and the curriculum map for portfolio guidance for future PPS cohorts. Adapting and updating this guidance based on teacher reflections and stakeholder feedback will ensure that best practice keeps evolving.

Reporting to parents

Your school will have established mechanisms and procedures for reporting on student progress to parents. There are several factors to consider when deciding on your approach to this within the PPS course. The following diagram shows some of the questions you might consider with the core team at your school. However, it is important to note that this is not an exhaustive list, and your school may already have reporting practices that differ from these.

Questions to consider

For DP/CP schools: Has a precedent already been set for PPS based on the current reporting process for theory of knowledge? If so, do you agree with that process as best practice, or would you report on PPS differently?

Does your school offer parents **live-time reporting** of assessment grades each term/semester? If so, does the PPS course need to match the expectation of providing an assessment grade at intervals, or could you deliver feedback in a different way at different times?

What might a PPS report look like? Consider:

- a teacher-written comment on term/semester performance and future goals/next steps for improvement
- student reflection on their growth, challenges, goals for the future and how they will achieve them
- a combination of student and teacher comments
- an extract of the student's portfolio with a commentary from the student and/or teacher.

Have parents been consulted on what they want to receive as a report on PPS progress?

Have students been consulted on how they think a report can be best constructed for PPS?

Could PPS progress be reported on as part of a wider CP core report, or should the components be kept separate for reporting purposes? Are all components of the CP core reported on in your school?

Top tip!

The purpose of having this discussion with key stakeholders within your school is to ensure that CP parents understand the learning taking place, their child's progress, and the next steps for their continued growth within PPS. Exploring these questions should stimulate conversation on best practices for reporting and allow the key stakeholders in your school community to make the best decision on reporting for your context.

Commitment to success

Assessment in PPS is not simply about ticking boxes – it is about guiding growth, reinforcing reflection and preparing students for the real world. When thoughtfully designed and delivered, assessment becomes a tool for empowerment, not just evaluation. Recognise that the skills measured in this course go beyond grades – they are life skills. Your approach to assessment can and should reflect the transformational nature of PPS.

Key takeaways: Chapter 8

- Use formative assessment for ongoing feedback and summative assessment for evaluation.
- Prioritise purpose over process. Every assessment – formative or summative – should help students better understand themselves, their skills and their goals.
- Use assessment formats that prepare students for the dynamic challenges of higher education and professional life (such as presentations, podcasts, debates) and vary them throughout the course.
- Grading scales should align with school policy and be meaningful to students and parents.
- Embrace feedback as learning. Timely, specific, and student-centred feedback should be at the heart of your assessment approach.
- Treat the portfolio as an evolving reflection of student voice and growth – something curated, not completed.
- Portfolio completion will be defined by your school, but it must meet IB requirements.
- Make reporting meaningful. Collaborate with students, parents, and your core team to ensure that reports communicate progress, potential, and purpose.
- Consult key stakeholders to design effective assessment, portfolio and reporting practices.

Key terms

grading scale: a system used to report levels of learner performance, often aligned with other components/subjects

live-time reporting: the practice of giving parents real-time notifications and feedback about assessments, etc., instead of delivering the information at particular fixed intervals

9 The student portfolio for personal and professional skills

This chapter covers the following:

- What is the personal and professional skills portfolio?
- Artefacts and annotations
- Portfolio development tool for students
- Portfolio evaluation tool for teachers

This chapter is intended for CP coordinators and PPS coordinators/teachers.

What is the personal and professional skills portfolio?

The personal and professional skills (PPS) portfolio is a valuable tool with two main uses.

1 A learning journey record

The portfolio allows students to compile and document their learning and growth throughout their PPS journey. This can be used to initiate discussions between the student and teacher, leading to a reflection on previous inquiries and a celebration of the progress that has taken place so far. It can also assist students in setting goals and addressing gaps in knowledge, understanding or skill application.

2 An indication of course completion

The portfolio is used to determine completion of the PPS course and to highlight students' achievements over the two years. It should capture, evidence and validate the learning that has taken place. However, that should not stop students from using their completed portfolios as inspiration for setting themselves goals beyond the Career-related Programme (CP). Encourage this practice to inspire students to become lifelong learners, both personally and professionally.

> **Top tip!**
>
> The PPS portfolio can be invaluable for students when completing their university applications. In it, students can:
>
> - reflect upon their growth and share their successes in university admissions essays and/or personal statements
> - create a narrative of their CP experiences as they prepare for university admissions interviews (or interviews for internships/the workplace)
> - share stories of impactful learning experiences that have shaped them as a student/person
> - provide evidence of skills development and personal growth.

As you have seen, determining whether a student has successfully completed the PPS course is a school-based decision, informed by the IB requirements. Schools must establish clear criteria for portfolio completion and consistently communicate these expectations to all key stakeholders. Included in these criteria should be the ability to provide:

- artefacts that provide evidence of progression across all five learning outcomes
- artefacts that showcase development in at least four concepts
- artefacts that highlight growth in a variety of contexts
- **annotations** for each artefact that include details about the concept(s), context(s), content, skill(s) and learning outcome(s) that it relates to
- opportunities for student reflection throughout.

Artefacts and annotations

An artefact is any piece of evidence that demonstrates a student's progress towards or achievement of a specific learning outcome. Artefacts are symbols of student growth, providing a foundation for reflection and assessment. The following graphic offers some ideas for what artefacts might be, but there are many others.

When considering what kinds of artefacts are commonly used in your school, think about the format(s) you recommend for the overall portfolio. Schools can be as flexible or as prescriptive as they wish with this, either recommending a specific format, such as a particular digital application or a paper-based portfolio, or allowing students to choose how to compile their portfolio themselves. Any decision made on your school's accepted portfolio format(s) will impact the kind of artefacts your students include. Consider this as you formulate your approach to best practice in artefact curation in your school's context.

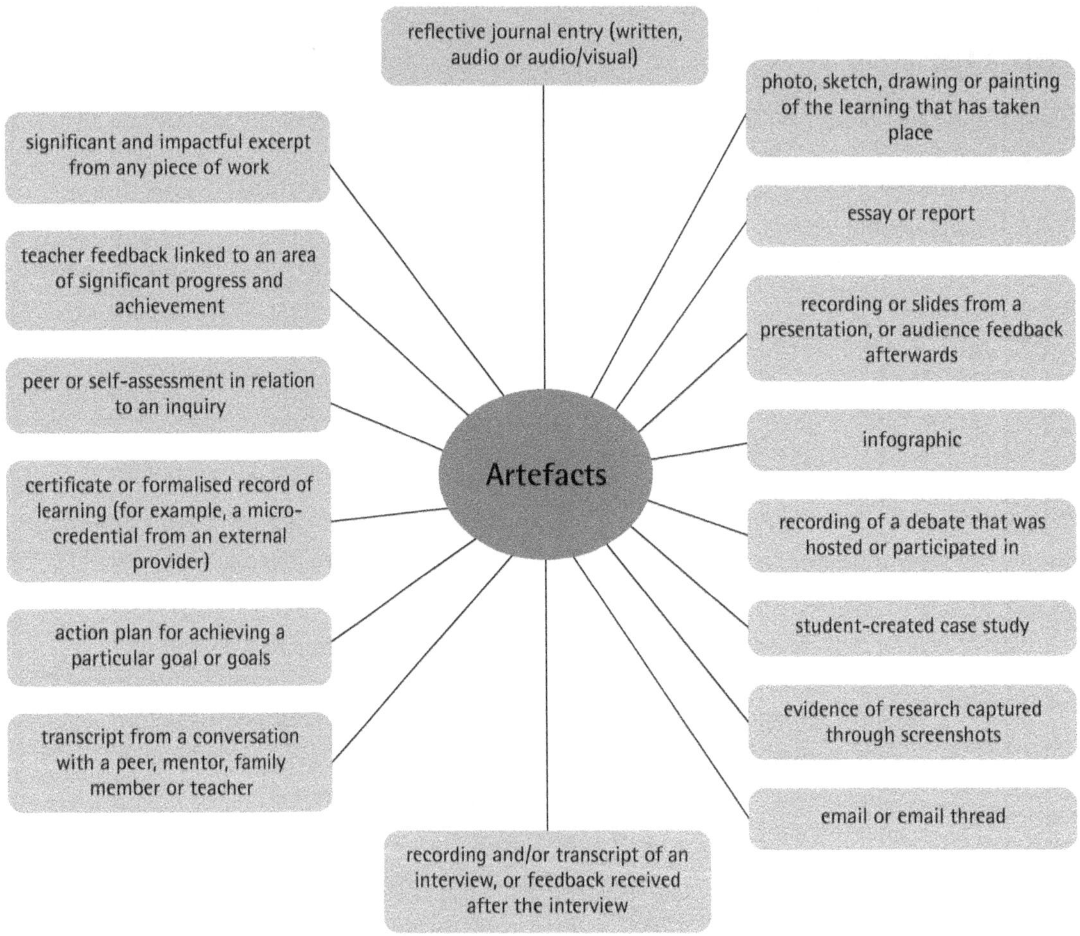

Regardless of the portfolio format(s) in use, schools should offer students guidance on what an artefact must achieve with its inclusion. A usable artefact should:

- represent some progress towards one or more of the learning outcomes
- be accompanied by an annotation, providing details on the concept(s), context(s), content, skill(s) and learning outcome(s) that it relates to
- be meaningful to the student
- highlight progress and development over the two-year course
- display deep personal engagement with the learning that has taken place
- support the student in meeting the IB and school-based requirements for completion of PPS
- encourage reflection on the impact of this learning by the student.

This list should serve as a starting point for discussions between CP staff at your school as you create your student guidance on artefact curation.

Example

Let's explore what an artefact from one of the example inquiries from Chapter 7 might look like: Ethical decision-making in the digital age.

Inquiry title	Description	Concepts	Contexts	Skills	Learning outcomes
Ethical decision-making in the digital age	Investigating ethical dilemmas in digital spaces, including AI, social media, and data privacy.	Systems Perspectives	Career-related study Reflective project Professional life	Ethical decision-making Critical thinking Communication Information literacy	LO2, LO3, LO5

The following is written from a student's perspective.

Artefact: A video of a class debate on an ethical dilemma, with me as the host

Annotation: This video artefact shows me posing an ethical dilemma to my peers and then hosting the ensuing debate. I devised the ethical dilemma and split my classmates into two groups, giving each group a specific perspective to represent. I allowed each group time to research their perspective and prepare before starting the debate. The ethical dilemma was 'Should artificial intelligence (AI) be used in any capacity when decisions directly impact human safety?'

This learning experience and my chosen artefact relate to the Systems and Perspectives concepts we explored within this inquiry. It is also highly relevant (and interesting!) to me, as I am studying engineering for my CRS, with a view to specialising in automotive or aeronautical engineering at university. This activity is therefore also relevant to my preparations for my reflective project and future professional life. The skills I am developing here are ethical decision-making, critical thinking and communication. This activity has helped me progress towards the following PPS learning outcomes:

- LO2: Develop and apply communication and interpersonal skills in various contexts.
- LO3: Develop and apply thinking skills in a variety of contexts.
- LO5: Demonstrate an awareness of the ethical implications of one's choices and actions on self and others.

Reflection and impact: As you can see from the video, this was great fun! I was pleased to see my classmates invested in this ethical dilemma. I was initially worried that they wouldn't find it interesting as they are all studying Music, Business and Sports CRS pathways, but it turned out better than I had hoped for. I really enjoyed posing challenging and probing questions to my peers to push their thinking and have them critically examine the points they were using to defend their perspective in this ethical dilemma. Listening to their responses opened my mind to different ways of thinking about this ethical dilemma and deepened my understanding of this issue.

What seems daunting to me, though, is that I might need to put forward my thoughts on this within the workplace in just a few years.

I found it quite challenging to host the debate without letting my biases and perspective on the ethical dilemma come through in my words and mannerisms. After watching the video back, I think I will focus on learning how to better manage my facial expressions when listening to perspectives I disagree with, so it isn't so obvious in the future. This can make me a better, more neutral listener, and I think it will benefit me personally and professionally in building and maintaining relationships. I also think it will help me when writing my reflective project as I try to make sure my bias doesn't seep into everything I write! We have an upcoming student-led inquiry in a couple of months, and I will discuss this with my teacher as a potential focus.

Portfolio development tool for students

This development tool is designed to help students structure their portfolio by documenting their inquiry-based learning process, skills development, learning outcomes achieved, and connections to PPS concepts and contexts. By completing this tool for each inquiry, students will have well-documented reflections that demonstrate their growth and achievements.

Student information

Name: ____________________

Date: ____________________

Career-related study (CRS): ____________________

1. Inquiry overview

Title of inquiry: ____________________

Inquiry focus question: ____________________

Concept(s) explored (tick all that apply):

- ❑ Change
- ❑ Connections
- ❑ Identities
- ❑ Perspectives
- ❑ Systems
- ❑ Wellbeing

Explain, giving examples, how each of the identified concepts were explored through your inquiry:

____

____

____

Context(s) explored (tick all that apply):

- ❑ Career-related study
- ❑ Community engagement
- ❑ Diploma Programme courses
- ❑ Language and cultural studies
- ❑ Reflective project
- ❑ Informal learning
- ❑ Personal life
- ❑ Professional life

Describe where each of the selected contexts are explored through your inquiry:

____

____

____

Examples of content explored (such as personal goal-setting, ethics in professional settings, digital footprint awareness, workplace leadership strategies).

____

____

2. Inquiry-based learning process

FOCUS:

(How did you identify your inquiry focus? What motivated this exploration?)

____

____

____

EXPLORE:

(What sources of information did you use? How did you expand your understanding of the topic?)

- ❑ Conducted research (articles, books, case studies)
- ❑ Conducted interviews with professionals
- ❑ Participated in discussions and debates
- ❑ Engaged in workplace observation
- ❑ Other: ______________________________________

ACT:

(What actions did you take to develop your skills? How did you apply what you learned?)

- ❑ Created a project, presentation, or written reflection
- ❑ Engaged in real-world problem-solving
- ❑ Applied skills in a community engagement setting

- ❑ Collaborated with peers or mentors
- ❑ Other: ____________________

REFLECT:

What did you learn from this inquiry? What challenges did you face, and how did you overcome them?

____

____

____

SHARE:

(How have you shared your learning? What impact has this inquiry had on your personal or professional growth?)

- ❑ Created a digital portfolio entry
- ❑ Presented findings to peers, mentors, or a professional audience
- ❑ Wrote a blog, article, or reflection
- ❑ Shared insights with a wider community
- ❑ Other: ____________________

3. Learning outcomes checklist

(Tick all learning outcomes demonstrated in this inquiry.)

- ❑ LO1: Develop and apply intrapersonal skills in a variety of contexts.
  Examples: self-awareness, resilience, time management.
- ❑ LO2: Develop and apply communication and interpersonal skills in a variety of contexts.
  Examples: teamwork, leadership, conflict resolution.
- ❑ LO3: Develop and apply thinking skills in a variety of contexts.
  Examples: critical thinking, problem-solving, ethical reasoning.
- ❑ LO4: Develop and apply intercultural understanding in a variety of contexts.
  Examples: cultural awareness, empathy, social responsibility.
- ❑ LO5: Demonstrate an awareness of the ethical implications of one's choices and actions on self and others.
  Examples: ethical decision-making, understanding impact, responsibility.

4. Skills development checklist

(Tick the specific skills you developed in this inquiry.)

Intrapersonal skills:

- ❑ Adaptability
- ❑ Reflection and reflexivity
- ❑ Resilience
- ❑ Self-advocacy
- ❑ Self-awareness
- ❑ Self-management

Interpersonal skills:

- ❑ Change management and conflict mediation
- ❑ Collaboration and networking
- ❑ Communication
- ❑ Leadership

Thinking skills:

- ❑ Critical thinking
- ❑ Creative thinking
- ❑ Ethical decision-making
- ❑ Information literacy
- ❑ Problem-solving
- ❑ Reflection and reflexivity
- ❑ Systems thinking

Intercultural understanding:

- ❑ Change management and conflict mediation
- ❑ Civic and social responsibility
- ❑ Empathy
- ❑ Ethics and personal values
- ❑ Reflection and reflexivity
- ❑ Self-efficacy
- ❑ Social awareness

5. Evidence submission

(Attach or link evidence related to your inquiry.)

Primary Artefact (for example, project, essay, video, presentation): ______________________

Supporting Evidence (for example, notes, research, feedback, reflections): ______________________

Annotation of artefact: ______________________

Teacher or mentor feedback: ______________________

6. Future growth and next steps

What would you like to explore further? How will this inquiry support your future academic or professional development?

____

____

____

Portfolio evaluation tool for teachers

This evaluation tool is designed to help you monitor and evaluate students' portfolios by assessing their inquiry-based learning process, skills development, achievement of learning outcomes, and connections to PPS concepts and contexts. By using this tool throughout the personal and professional skills course, you can track students' progress, provide formative feedback and determine whether students have successfully met the course requirements. This structured evaluation ensures that each portfolio provides clear evidence of student growth, reflection, and achievement in alignment with IB expectations.

How to use this tool

- Use Section 2 to monitor student progress throughout the PPS course.
- Use Section 3 to check if the student meets all required learning outcomes.
- Use Section 4 to evaluate the final completed portfolio.
- Use Section 5 to determine whether the portfolio meets IB requirements for successful completion.
- Use Section 6 to provide feedback and specify any revisions that are required before final submission.

1. Student information

Student name: ______________________

Teacher name: ______________________

Review date: ______________________

Career-related study (CRS): ______________________

2. Portfolio monitoring checklist

Use this section for periodic portfolio reviews throughout the PPS course.

Portfolio requirement	Check (✓) if complete	Comments/notes
Portfolio contains multiple well-documented inquiries.		
Entries include a clear focus question guiding each inquiry.		
Student has explored at least four concepts from the PPS course.		
Entries demonstrate engagement in at least two different contexts.		
Portfolio provides evidence of skill development across all four skill domains.		
Reflections are substantive and demonstrate critical thought.		
Artefacts and supporting evidence are clearly documented.		
Student has regularly engaged in self-reflection on progress.		

Additional notes:

___

___

___

3. Portfolio learning outcomes review

Use this section to track progress towards PPS learning outcomes.

Learning outcome	Demonstrated? (✔)	Comments/evidence
LO1: Develop and apply intrapersonal skills in a variety of contexts.		
LO2: Develop and apply communication and interpersonal skills in a variety of contexts.		
LO3: Develop and apply thinking skills in a variety of contexts.		
LO4: Develop and apply intercultural understanding in a variety of contexts.		
LO5: Demonstrate an awareness of the ethical implications of one's choices and actions on self and others.		

Does the portfolio provide sufficient evidence that all five learning outcomes have been met?

- ❑ Yes
- ❑ No (specify required revisions below)

Required revisions (if applicable):

___

___

___

___

___

___

___

___

___

___

___

4. Portfolio evaluation rubric

For final assessment of the complete PPS portfolio.

Criteria	Exemplary	Proficient	Developing	Needs Improvement
Depth of inquiry	Inquiry questions are insightful and lead to deep learning.	Inquiry questions are clear and meaningful.	Inquiry questions are somewhat generic.	Inquiry questions are vague or lacking.
Concept and context integration	Concepts and contexts are explored meaningfully and connected well.	Concepts and contexts are explored adequately.	Concepts and contexts are somewhat connected.	Little connection to concepts and contexts.
Skill development	Evidence of strong skill development across all domains.	Evidence of skill development in key PPS areas.	Limited skill development shown.	No clear evidence of skill development.
Reflection and growth	Reflections show deep critical thinking and meaningful insights.	Reflections are clear and show personal connection.	Reflections are present but lack depth.	Minimal or no reflection provided.
Presentation and organisation	Portfolio is well-organised, professional, and easy to navigate.	Portfolio is organised with minor issues.	Portfolio is partially organised and somewhat clear.	Portfolio is disorganised or difficult to navigate.

5. Determining completion

To achieve successful completion of the PPS course, the student's portfolio must evidence the following:

Requirement	Met? (✔)	Comments/evidence
Knowledge and understanding of a minimum of four concepts.		
Development and application of at least two skills from each skill domain (eight skills in total).		
Each of those skills applied in a minimum of two contexts over the course of study.		
Progress and growth in relation to all five learning outcomes.		
Demonstrated student reflection on learning throughout the portfolio.		

Has the student successfully met all PPS course requirements?

- ❑ Yes
- ❑ No (specify required revisions below)

Required final revisions (if applicable):

____

____

____

6. Final portfolio status

- ❑ Meets PPS portfolio requirements
- ❑ Requires final revisions (listed above)

7. Final comments and next steps

Strengths observed in the portfolio:

____

____

____

Areas for improvement or final revisions needed:

____

____

____

____

____

____

____

____

____

____

____

____

____

____

____

Commitment to success

A strong PPS portfolio is not a checklist of tasks – it is a reflection of the student's personal and professional journey. It captures growth, celebrates learning and prepares students to articulate who they are and where they are going. To support portfolio success:

- champion authenticity – encourage students to curate artefacts that genuinely matter to them and which tell their unique story of growth
- embed reflection early and often – help students understand that reflection is not something that happens at the end, but a tool for growth throughout the inquiry process
- balance structure with flexibility – provide clear guidance and expectations while allowing students space to personalise the format and content
- prioritise quality over quantity – a smaller number of meaningful, well-annotated artefacts is far more powerful than a large volume of loosely connected evidence
- use the portfolio as a learning tool, not just a final product – revisit it throughout the course to celebrate milestones, adjust goals, and strengthen students' sense of purpose.

When educators commit to thoughtful scaffolding, consistent guidance and a belief in the value of student voice, the PPS portfolio becomes more than a requirement – it becomes a powerful launchpad for future success.

Key takeaways: Chapter 9

- The PPS student portfolio serves both as a record of growth and a tool for determining course completion.
- Artefacts must evidence progress across learning outcomes.
- Annotations are essential; they link artefacts to the relevant learning outcomes, concepts, contexts and skills and tell the story of how this learning was impactful to the student.
- Portfolios can exist in a wide variety of formats if they meet IB and school-defined criteria.
- A student portfolio development tool can be used to support the curation process and reflections throughout the PPS course.
- A portfolio evaluation tool can support teachers in monitoring progress, providing feedback and confirming course completion.
- Portfolio expectations can evolve based on student needs and cohort feedback.

Key term

annotation: a brief explanation that connects an artefact to the concepts, contexts, content, skills and learning outcomes

10 Personal and professional skills and links to the Career-related Programme and Diploma Programme cores

This chapter covers the following:

- Personal and professional skills and the Career-related Programme core
- Personal and professional skills and the Diploma Programme core

This chapter is intended for all staff involved in the implementation of the Career-related Programme (CP) core and the Diploma Programme (DP) core.

Personal and professional skills and the Career-related Programme core

The CP core components are designed to work together, with common threads and shared terminology throughout to ensure a holistic experience and exploration of essential skills and concepts. The diagram below shows some of the connections between the core components.

The collaborative activities outlined below will enable CP core staff to support integration between the personal and professional skills (PPS) course and the other core components. There are also some example activities for students, which showcase the links between PPS and the other core components, as they participate in meaningful learning engagements.

Spot the similarity

This activity helps CP core staff become familiar with all the components of the CP. This will enable everyone to work collaboratively to make any links explicit and to carefully scaffold development in these areas across the CP core. The activity works best when done at the beginning of the CP journey, when staff are planning their core delivery for the first time.

- **Step 1:** Have the staff responsible for each CP core component produce and present a concise summary of their component for the wider team, taking into consideration the learning outcomes/assessment objectives, skills and concepts covered.
- **Step 2:** While listening to the summaries presented by their colleagues, staff should identify any similarities in the skills and concepts between the component being presented and their own.
- **Step 3:** Having identified the similarities, staff should work together to co-design how and when the learning in this area will occur within the respective components. Staff should scaffold the learning to ensure that students experience only intentional overlap and can undertake activities, projects and inquiries that expand across components, highlighting the explicit links between the identified skills and concepts.

The audit

This activity reinforces a familiarity with the different components for staff in each area, but works better for schools that have been offering the CP for some time and are looking to create a stronger alignment and connection between the four components.

- **Step 1:** Have staff share curriculum maps, timelines and other documents that highlight what they cover and when. They should work together to audit all documentation and highlight common threads between components.
- **Step 2:** Encourage staff to explore how those skills and concepts are developed discreetly in each component. They should identify **unintentional overlaps** or any areas where work is being duplicated.
- **Step 3:** Encourage staff to work collaboratively to redesign areas of unintentional overlap to make the overall implementation of the CP core more cohesive and time efficient. This involves maximising the available learning hours and hopefully encouraging more profound learning.
- **Step 4:** Ask staff to reorder learning to better scaffold the student experience. For example, if the same skill or concept is explored across two or more components, the process could be structured as a **spiralling progression** across the components, building on the learning that has already occurred and being exposed to increasingly more complex and/or contextualised activities and inquiries.

Top tip!

Normalise identifying the links between the core components in the following ways.

- Encourage core staff to consistently use statements such as: 'Building upon your learning from PPS/RP/LCS/CE, let's continue to explore [skill/concept] in greater depth/a different context.'
- Share and reference the learning outcomes/assessment objectives for all components related to the skills and concepts that are being developed.
- Provide a reflection prompt for students in their PPS portfolio that asks them to consider whether and how other components contributed to their progression in the area they were evidencing.
- Design inquiries that go across the core components and are supported by staff from the different components. This will help students see the links across the core clearly.

Example

Student activity: Personal and professional skills and the reflective project

Structured debates on ethical dilemmas related to students' career interests are an effective way to prepare them for the reflective project (RP). In this activity, students can select an ethical dilemma from their chosen career field and pose it to their classmates as a formal debate.

The student hosting the debate should ask probing questions (not **leading questions**) and aim to extract as many different perspectives and thoughts on their chosen ethical dilemma as possible. If a mixture of opinions and viewpoints does not occur naturally within the class, the host student can assign perspectives to groups and allow them research time before the debate begins. At the end of the debate, the student hosting should state their stance and justify why they think this way.

This activity sharpens students' ability to construct well-reasoned arguments, examine bias and differing perspectives, and make ethical decisions, which are key skills in both the PPS course and the RP. The debate task also helps each student gain insights into how their peers view their ethical dilemma, which may inspire new lines of inquiry for their continued research.

Top tip!

Consider doing the debate activity twice – once near the beginning of CP 1 and once near the end of CP 1. This can provide an interesting reflection point for students, as they examine how their intercultural understanding, knowledge and understanding of bias, and ethical decision-making have improved. This could even lead to a curated portfolio entry that speaks to this development.

Example 1

Student activity: Personal and professional skills and language and cultural studies

Reading *The Culture Map* by Erin Meyer and exploring it through follow-up activities is an excellent way to harmonise linguistic, cultural and communicative learning between PPS and language and cultural studies. Students can carry out the following tasks.

Participate in a group discussion: Highlight their key learning, pose questions for the group, and explain how they can begin to adapt their communications to be more effective when building or maintaining personal and professional relationships across cultures. Alternatively, students could present this information through a book report, journal entry or video reflection if they prefer.

Create a script: Act out some concepts and examples explored in the book within their personal or professional contexts. Students could show examples of varying levels of proficiency in cross-cultural communication, teaching one another key concepts from the book and sharing effective practices.

Engage in further research: Design a student-led inquiry on an area of linguistic or cultural learning that they have been inspired to examine further by their reading.

These activities ensure that students learn about cultural and linguistic diversity and practise applying this knowledge in personal and professional contexts. Throughout this process, students engage in learning that highlights the explicit links between PPS and LCS and supports their development in both components.

Example 2

Student activity: Personal and professional skills and community engagement

An effective way to explicitly link PPS and community engagement (CE) is through a shared inquiry focused on a community needs assessment. In this activity, students work in groups and collaborate with community members to identify the needs of the local community by conducting surveys, interviews and secondary research. The results of this work can support students in determining the next steps for their CE journey, while developing their research, communication and leadership skills.

You can assign students specific roles, such as project manager, interviewer or data analyst, to encourage teamwork and to highlight how professional skills translate into real-world impact. After gathering data, students can present their findings and propose realistic, actionable projects that respond to the community's needs.

This activity helps students develop empathy, understand diverse perspectives and see how ethical reasoning informs responsible action – all key skills in both PPS and CE. It also encourages students to examine how their personal interests connect with the broader needs of a community, fostering a sense of social responsibility.

Personal and professional skills and the Diploma Programme core

Although the PPS component of the CP core is not specifically designed to be connected to the DP core, there are still opportunities for collaboration between the two. Obviously, this is only applicable to schools that offer both IB programmes.

The information below primarily focuses on the connections between the PPS and **theory of knowledge (TOK)** components, although additional ideas for collaboration across other CP and DP core components are also explored.

Personal and professional skills and the theory of knowledge

PPS and the TOK share some similarities. We have chosen the following three aspects to provide examples of how students and staff might collaborate through valuable learning opportunities that meet the needs of both components:

- critical thinking and reflection
- intercultural understanding and perspectives
- ethical thinking.

Example

Student activity: Critical thinking and reflection

Students can engage in a case study analysis titled 'Interpreting evidence: Whose truth matters?' to develop critical thinking and reflection. In this activity, groups of PPS and TOK students can analyse a controversial real-world case, such as:

- differing media reports on a global event
- scientific studies with conflicting outcomes
- historical events interpreted from various perspectives.

TOK students can question the reliability and validity of the evidence presented, while PPS students can assess how these interpretations affect decision-making in professional contexts, such as journalism, healthcare or policymaking.

The groups then present their findings, highlighting how different interpretations of the same evidence can lead to different conclusions and actions.

The activity concludes with a reflective discussion, in which students evaluate the impact of bias, perspective and context.

Example

Student activity: Intercultural understanding and perspectives

Students could participate in a cross-cultural interview project titled 'Cultural lenses: understanding our differences'.

In this activity, groups of PPS and TOK students conduct interviews with individuals from diverse cultural backgrounds, such as classmates, teachers, friends and family, and other local community members, focusing on their perspectives regarding global issues such as education, rights and inclusion, environmental sustainability, and cultural preservation. TOK students can analyse how cultural backgrounds and experiences shape knowledge and beliefs, while PPS students can examine how these cultural differences influence communication, collaboration and professional interactions.

After conducting the interviews, both groups of students should work together to compare and contrast the responses, identifying common themes, differences and the underlying cultural influences that shape these perspectives. They should then deliver their findings through a live presentation, video or written report, explaining how understanding diverse cultural viewpoints can improve global cooperation and professional relationships.

The activity concludes with a class discussion on how intercultural understanding can help foster empathy, reduce bias and enhance effective communication in personal and professional contexts.

Top tip!

Try contacting other CP schools around the world to see if they would like to be involved in the interviews. This would offer a greater diversity of cultures and backgrounds, while fostering new CP connections and a greater professional network for your students and staff.

Example

Student activity: Ethical thinking

Students can participate in an ethical dilemma simulation titled 'What should we do?' Within mixed PPS/TOK groups, students take on the role of different stakeholders in scenarios, such as a business debating releasing a product with uncertain environmental impacts but excellent profit potential. TOK students can analyse the scenario from the standpoint of ethical knowledge questions, while PPS students can apply ethical decision-making frameworks to find a solution. Each group then presents solutions, justifying their decisions through knowledge, reasoning and professional ethics. A reflective discussion follows, helping students understand the importance of ethical thinking in real-world contexts.

Top tip

Teachers can use generative AI to help identify the ethical dilemmas, create specific simulations and outline the stakeholders involved. They can also make the simulations increasingly complex to test students' ability to make a reasonable decision with a clear justification.

Wider Career-related Programme and Diploma Programme core links

PPS is not the only CP core component that offers collaboration points with the DP core. Consider how your RP and extended essay (EE) coordinators could work together to establish best practices for both components (if the role is not already combined). This could be in areas such as – but not limited to – academic integrity, research skills, academic and professional writing, reflections and teaching essential self-management skills critical to the successful completion of long-term academic projects. Likewise, **creativity, activity, service (CAS)** and CE coordinators can support each other in establishing agreements with local organisations, developing community partnerships, and creating protocols that govern how school community members learn from, learn with and contribute to the communities they interact with.

Commitment to success

The power of the CP core lies in its integration. PPS, the RP, language and cultural skills (LCS), and CE are not separate entities, but interconnected opportunities for growth. If you are an IB educator in a DP/CP school, you may also have the chance to build bridges across the DP and CP cores, helping students to meaningfully connect across programmes. Embrace these links and opportunities. Use them to create coherence, enrich learning, and support each student in becoming a more capable and confident student.

Key takeaways: Chapter 10

- PPS links naturally to the RP, LCS, and CE through shared skills, concepts, and ethical and/or cultural learning opportunities.
- Activities such as structured debates, cross-cultural communication tasks, and community needs assessments can be used to build clear bridges across the CP core components.
- CP core staff can strengthen the integration of all components through collaborative audits, co-planning and consistent use of shared terminology.
- In DP/CP schools, PPS and TOK students can collaborate through inquiry-based tasks on critical thinking, ethical reasoning and intercultural understanding. These interactions can support students both in developing skills for PPS and in preparing for their RP.

Key terms

creativity, activity, service (CAS): a component of the DP core where students engage in experiences that foster personal and interpersonal development

leading questions: questions that are phrased in a way that suggests or encourages a particular answer

spiralling progression: a scaffolded approach where students revisit skills and/or concepts across components at increasing levels of complexity

theory of knowledge (TOK): a component of the DP core that encourages students to explore how knowledge is constructed and understood

unintentional overlap: the repetition of similar content or skills across core components without deliberate coordination, potentially reducing efficiency or impact

11 Supporting the student's reflective project journey

This chapter covers the following:

- What is the reflective project?
- Connections between the reflective project and the Career-related Programme framework
- The supervisor's role in supporting students through the reflective project learning journey
- Reflective project moderation and standardisation practice

This chapter is intended for reflective project (RP) supervisors, RP coordinators and Career-related Programme (CP) coordinators.

What is the reflective project?

The RP is a compulsory part of the CP. It is an independent, research-based project in which students explore an ethical dilemma within a career field of their choosing, to produce an externally assessed project. As a culminating experience carried out across the two years of the CP, students demonstrate many of the skills gained throughout their CP learning journey through the RP.

Student voice and agency are also central to the RP, as they make their own decisions about various factors, including their career field, ethical dilemma, research question and how they want to present their work (written, audio, visual or audio-video format). Students develop and apply critical thinking, research and professional communication skills, while considering different perspectives and contexts related to their chosen ethical dilemma and career field.

Students work closely with a supervisor and have the chance to think like a future career practitioner, developing skills that will benefit them in both their further education and career.

The following table outlines some of the key requirements of the RP.

Key aspect	Details
Focus	Must explore an ethical dilemma related to a career area.
Format	Can be submitted in various formats (written, audio, visual, audio-visual).
Length	Up to 4,000 words in total, including a written reflective statement of up to 1,000 words.
Time	Requires a minimum of 50 hours of independent work.
Supervision	Students will receive 3–6 hours of support from their RP supervisor (including viva voce).
Presentation	Students will present their research findings to get feedback after their first draft.
Viva voce	At the end, students will participate in a concluding interview with their supervisor.

Assessment	The RP is submitted to the IB for assessment. It is assessed using five criteria that are aligned with assessment objectives.
Passing requirement	Students must achieve at least a D grade to be awarded the IB CP Certificate.

According to the IB guidance, the aims of the RP are for students to:

- engage in personal inquiry
- develop critical thinking and research skills to explore an ethical dilemma
- seek and appreciate local and/or global perspectives
- appraise the reliability and bias of resources found during the research process
- develop effective communication skills by creating a structured, coherent and balanced argument
- develop self-management skills to support the research and product-creation process
- engage in ongoing reflective practice.

You can see how the RP connects with other elements of the CP framework, and how these connections can contribute to students' RP learning journey and success.

The RP is usually introduced a few months into the first year of the CP, and submitted within the second year (depending on your school's timetable). Students should utilise knowledge and skills acquired across their whole experience of the CP. The RP provides schools with a fantastic opportunity to intentionally build connections across the CP core components, Diploma Programme (DP) subjects, and the career-related studies (CRS).

Connections between the reflective project and the Career-related Programme framework

As shown in Chapter 3, there are intricate connections between the RP and other components of the CP framework. The RP is an excellent opportunity for students to apply what they have learned from their entire CP experience and showcase their growth in critical and ethical thinking, communication and intercultural understanding.

Throughout this resource, as well as in your engagement with the CP framework, you have probably noticed that each component offers a variety of opportunities to identify ethical dilemmas, enhance students' ethical thinking and decision-making skills, and improve their intercultural understanding. These connections to each component will now be explored more closely.

Community engagement

Community engagement (CE) activities offer students the chance to apply and transfer the knowledge and skills learned in the classroom to real-world scenarios. These experiences help students understand complex community needs, engage in social interactions, and appreciate diverse perspectives.

Students may have encountered real-life ethical dilemmas during their CE experiences. For example, they might have identified unethical treatment of refugees in their community, or seen power imbalances through which minority voices are overlooked. These experiences will help students identify ethical issues and understand their impact on various communities. These experiences encourage students to reflect and deepen their understanding of how individuals and communities are interconnected, both locally and globally. This experience supports several essential aspects of the RP – identifying an ethical dilemma and exploring different perspectives and contexts in which the dilemma is manifested.

The RP encourages students to think like a future practitioner, and the practical nature of CE can help them see the real-life application of their research. Sound ethical decisions require research, thinking routines and effective communication. As such, students may want to consider involving stakeholders from their CE activities to enable them to include diverse perspectives through surveys, questionnaires and interviews as part of their research.

Language and cultural studies

Language and cultural studies (LCS) provides a valuable cultural lens for examining ethical dilemmas. By exploring how language and culture shape identities and perspectives, students can discover new connections and ways of engaging with different viewpoints. Analysing written materials, dialogues and narratives can reveal similarities and differences between cultures. For example, through LCS, students might find that eastern cultures view freedom of expression differently than western cultures, which could inform the perspectives they choose to explore for their RP.

Understanding linguistic and cultural contexts enhances students' appreciation of how ethical dilemmas are manifested and interpreted. By reflecting on their own and others' positionality in language and cultural studies, students can improve their intercultural understanding, critical reflection and reflexivity as they explore their ethical dilemmas.

Personal and professional skills

The personal and professional skills and RP components are intrinsically linked, as much of the skills development that takes place in PPS will significantly benefit students by preparing them for the RP. Students' experience in the PPS course is crucial for developing their ability to conduct comprehensive research and engage in the type of reflective practice required in the RP. Throughout the PPS course, students will also develop essential skills such as self-management, communication, collaboration and critical thinking. Such skills are vital for navigating the extended RP process and creating a research-based product that demonstrates their knowledge and understanding.

Ethics serve as a guiding principle in the personal and professional skills course, connecting directly to key concepts such as connections, identities, perspectives and systems. As you have seen, by incorporating these concepts into PPS inquiries, students will learn to understand ethics in various contexts and how they relate to personal and professional choices and actions. PPS also provides a crucial foundation for understanding ethical and responsible use of technology, including artificial intelligence, which students may encounter as both a research tool and as the subject of ethical dilemmas in their chosen career fields.

Additionally, the various artefacts and text types that students encounter during the PPS course will familiarise them with multimodal formats and options for communication of ideas (for example, written essays, business plans, presentations, videos, audio and multimedia products). These experiences can support students' understanding of structural elements and stylistic conventions for different text types, enabling them to choose the most suitable format option for their RP.

Diploma Programme subjects

Students' DP subjects will complement their CRS and the overall CP experience; through these subjects, students can develop academic and research skills. The experience of completing internal assessments (IAs) for different subjects helps to hone students' research, analytical and communication skills, which can scaffold them through the steps and methodologies necessary for completing an extensive research project.

Learning from DP courses might also prompt students to consider the ethical dimensions of different careers or contexts. For example:

- the business management or digital societies course might help students examine how the hospitality industry adapts to the effects of artificial intelligence
- the psychology course might help with understanding the impact of mature topics and themes in children's television programmes or the impact of gaming addiction on young people's psyche.

DP courses across multiple subject areas increasingly address matters relating to ethical and responsible AI use, from computer science courses exploring algorithmic bias to business studies examining AI's impact on various traditional business models, providing students with disciplinary perspectives on technology ethics that can inform their RP explorations.

Career-related studies

Career-related studies provide specialised knowledge in a particular field, giving students insights into their specific career pathway. Through these real-world connections and authentic learning experiences, students can uncover ethical issues that might inspire their RPs. Students could interview their CRS teachers and mentors, many of whom will be active practitioners in their fields, to gain a deeper understanding of the historical context, impacted stakeholders and societal trends surrounding their identified ethical dilemma.

Top tip!

Aligning and connecting the students' learning from DP courses, CRS, and CP core components provides a unique preparation for their RP learning journey.

The RP can also be a useful tool for students in the university admissions process. Their work could be submitted as an example of their engagement with the area of their chosen undergraduate degree or could provide an interesting discussion point for any admissions interview.

The supervisor's role in supporting students through the reflective project learning journey

The RP supervisor plays a pivotal role in supporting and guiding students through their RP learning journey. As educators, understanding the full scope of supervision responsibilities enables supervisors to provide effective mentorship while maintaining appropriate boundaries, ensuring that the supervision process supports students meaningfully and that their Reflective Project remains authentically their own work.

Supervisors dedicate 3-6 hours of focused time to support each student, including regular meetings, feedback sessions, and a concluding interview (the viva voce). This time should be strategically distributed across the five phases of the student's RP learning journey.

The primary responsibility of an RP supervisor is to keep students engaged and motivated over the extended timeline while ensuring they stay on the right path in terms of their ethical analysis, project development and understanding of the assessment criteria. Most importantly, timely feedback helps students build essential skills – self-management, research, social, thinking and communication skills – while helping them realise the significance of their research, understanding and thinking processes.

The five phases of supervision in the RP learning journey

Phase 1: Preparation and planning phase (Months 1–2)

Supervisor focus: Building foundations and establishing direction

During this crucial initial phase, the supervisor's primary role is to help students develop the knowledge and skills necessary for success during their project planning phase.

Supervisory responsibilities

- Check that students understand ethics and its relation to their career-related field or subject of study.
- Explain the nature and requirements of the RP while promoting student agency and empowering them to take ownership of their learning journey.
- Discuss the most appropriate research methods for the project.
- Guide students through the formal requirements for completing the project while supporting their self-management skills development.
- Host an initial supervisory meeting to help students complete their RP proposal form by:
  - facilitating discussion to devise well-formulated and focused research questions
  - helping establish objectives and rationale for their projects
  - supporting plans for collecting resources and research methodologies.
- Provide constructive feedback on project proposals while ensuring students understand feedback and how to apply it. A sample project proposal has been provided in the Appendix.
- Ensure students understand the assessment criteria and academic integrity expectations.
- Guide and facilitate peer feedback opportunities.
- Discuss different RP format options and encourage students to choose formats that best fit their interests and skills.

Supporting learner development

- Encourage students to come prepared to meetings with questions and initial ideas about their career interests.
- Foster openness about their interests and career aspirations.
- Support them in sharing draft proposals and research questions for feedback.
- Guide them in taking initiative for scheduling meetings and maintaining communication.
- Emphasise the importance of documenting discussions and feedback in their learning journals.
- Help them take ownership of project timelines and milestones.

Key activities and milestones to support students on

- Brainstorming sessions to identify ethical dilemmas within career fields
- Review and refinement of research questions through structured discussion
- Guidance on format options and their specific requirements
- Creation of realistic project timelines and milestones
- Exploration of available resources and appropriate research methodologies
- Submission of project proposals.

Phase 2: Research and analysis phase (Months 3–6)

Supervisor focus: Supporting independent research while ensuring academic integrity and ethical guidelines.

As students dive into the research phase, the supervisor role shifts to monitoring progress, ensuring ethical research practices, and helping navigate research challenges while maintaining their focus on the exploration of ethical dilemmas.

Supervisory responsibilities

- Guide students to plan and undertake research for their RPs.
- Monitor students' progress to offer guidance where appropriate and to ensure authenticity of student work.
- Ensure students are familiar with the ethical guidelines for the RP, including ethical research practices and responsible use of artificial intelligence.
- Ensure students have access to exemplars, guides, and resources on referencing and writing.
- Confirm students understand the assessment criteria and conform to academic integrity principles throughout this phase.
- Hold both formal and informal meetings that enable students to complete milestone reflection activities in their learning journals.
- Guide students in the evaluation of sources for reliability and bias.
- Ensure the students' RPs maintain a focus on discussions around their ethical dilemmas in a variety of contexts.
- Encourage students to recognise differing perspectives in their ethical discussions including local and/or global perspectives.
- Reinforce and cultivate specific Approaches to Learning (ATL) skills throughout the process.

Supporting learner development

- Monitor students through regular contact for progress updates without being overly directive.
- Provide guidance when students encounter research obstacles or ethical concerns.
- Encourage students to share interesting findings and emerging insights.
- Support students in evaluating conflicting sources or perspectives.
- Emphasise the importance of detailed record-keeping in learning journals.
- Help students take responsibility for their own work while maintaining pride in their developing projects.

Key activities and milestones to support students on

- Identification of gaps in research or perspective analysis
- Consideration of alternative research methods or sources when facing obstacles
- Management of large amounts of information
- Navigation through research setbacks or dead ends
- Meaningful reflection over the process and regular learning journal updates.

Phase 3: Development phase (Months 7–9)

Supervisor focus: Supporting research collation, analysis, synthesis and first draft development.

During the development phase, supervisors help students transform their research findings into coherent projects while ensuring they meet all requirements and maintain academic integrity throughout.

Supervisory responsibilities

- Provide feedback on students' approaches to synthesising research from multiple perspectives.
- Support students through the challenging process of organising complex information.
- Help ensure project structures support clear communication of ethical analyses.
- Monitor progress towards completing first drafts.
- Guide and confirm students' understanding of format-specific requirements and conventions.
- Ensure students develop and justify personal positions on their chosen ethical dilemmas.
- Continue to facilitate peer feedback sessions.
- Ensure students meet all RP requirements and align to assessment criteria.

Supporting student development

- Provide general guidance on students' drafts progression and completion.
- Provide clarification on format requirements and conventions.
- Offer feedback on clarity and logic of arguments.
- Support students through challenges in synthesising different perspectives on ethical dilemmas.
- Help maintain student momentum and motivation through this intensive and important phase.
- Encourage continued meaningful reflections in learning journals.

Key activities and milestones to support students on

- Completion of research analysis with multiple perspectives
- Organisation of findings into logical structures that maintain ethical focus
- Development of personal positions with supporting evidence
- Integration of feedback into draft development.

Phase 4: Presentation of findings (Months 10–11)

Supervisor focus: Preparing students for presentation and providing crucial feedback.

The presentation phase marks a critical transition point where supervisors help students articulate their thinking and prepare to communicate their research findings through oral presentations – a pivotal moment in the RP process.

Supervisory responsibilities

- Support students as they prepare their presentations of findings.
- Facilitate peer feedback following presentations.

- Provide developmental feedback to guide final revisions.
- Confirm students are on track for successful completion.
- Use assessment criteria to help students understand current performance levels.

Supporting student development

- Guide students to prepare thoroughly, ensuring they showcase their ethical analyses.
- Help students reflect on feedback and make informed decisions about revisions.
- Support students in using the feedback to create a complete full draft.
- Encourage clarifying questions about feedback, especially criteria-based comments.

Key activities and milestones to support students on

- Student presentation delivery (10 minutes maximum).
- Feedback collection from presentation audience.
- Student reflection on all feedback received.
- Preparation for final revision of the project draft.

Phase 5: Completion and submission phase (Months 11–12)

Supervisor focus: Final support, authentication, and celebration.

In the final phase, supervisors focus on supporting students through their final draft and revisions, providing feedback on their drafts, ensuring academic integrity, conducting the viva voce, and celebrating achievements.

Supervisory responsibilities

- Support students through final revisions.
- Review and provide criteria-based feedback on one full draft (your only formal review).*

> ***Important note for supervisors:** This is the only time you can provide formal feedback on a complete draft. You cannot edit student work directly but should offer suggestions, questions, and criteria-based feedback to guide improvements.

- Support students' final written reflection on the Final Reflection Form (FRF).
- Confirm authenticity of student work.
- Complete supervisor comments on students' Final Reflection Form (FRF).
- Report any plagiarism or suspicions of plagiarism to the CP coordinator.
- Conduct viva voce sessions with the aim of facilitating final reflections about RP processes and results.
- Complete predicted grades for students' completed projects.
- Support submission processes to the IB.
- Celebrate student achievements and reflect on their growth.

Supporting student development

- Encourage students to complete final revisions thoughtfully and independently.
- Support completion of final written reflection forms.
- Help students prepare for the viva voce by encouraging them to review their entire learning journey and leverage their learning journals.
- Ensure all submission requirements are met.
- Facilitate authentic participation in viva voce discussions, encouraging demonstration of understanding of ethical dilemmas and personal growth.

Key activities and milestones to support students on

- Final revision based on feedback received.
- Completion of final written reflection on the Final Reflection Form (FRF) (maximum 1,000 words).
- Final project submission in chosen formats and their requirements.
- Academic integrity check and authentication by supervisor.
- Viva voce preparation; student:
    - reviews entire learning journey using their RP learning journal
    - reflects on ethical dilemma evolution and personal position development
    - prepares to discuss research process, challenges, and discoveries.
- Viva voce interview (15–20 minute concluding interview) that includes:
    - focus of the RP and connection to career interest
    - how they identified their ethical dilemma and why it was chosen
    - initial thoughts and any bias and assumption changes regarding the dilemma
    - research undertaken and methodology reasoning
    - key research findings and format choice rationale
    - overall understanding of the ethical dilemma and personal position justification
    - perspective progression and skills development throughout the journey
    - self-evaluation of final project strengths and limitations
    - impact on future learning and career development.

(Sample viva voce sentence starters have been provided in the Appendix).

- Final authentication and IB submission.
- Celebration of achievement and reflection on growth.

Tips and strategies for successful RP supervision

Continuous support areas:

- Ensure students remain responsible for their own work while taking pride in developing products.
- Reinforce and cultivate Approaches to Learning (ATL) skills (self-management, research, social, thinking, and communication skills).
- Encourage students to ask for advice and information when needed.
- Monitor student progress to offer guidance and ensure authenticity of work.
- Encourage meaningful reflections and regular learning journal updates.
- Promote learning environments where students can offer and receive respectful feedback.
- Maintain focus on ethical frameworks and multiple perspectives throughout analyses.

Understanding supervision boundaries

Dos	Don'ts
✓ Provide guidance, suggestions, and feedback ✓ Ask probing questions to deepen student thinking ✓ Help students understand requirements and expectations ✓ Support students in finding appropriate resources and research methods ✓ Guide students in evaluating source reliability and bias	✗ Correct spelling or punctuation errors ✗ Make decisions on RP formats ✗ Correct information, data, or statistics ✗ Rewrite or reproduce any part of learner RPs ✗ Indicate where whole section might be better placed

Dos	Don'ts
✓ Facilitate feedback opportunities ✓ Encourage recognition of multiple perspectives and contexts ✓ Monitor student progress and authenticity of work ✓ Mark and provide criteria-based feedback on *only* one complete draft ✓ Conduct viva voce sessions	✗ Proofread student RPs for errors ✗ Correct bibliographies or citations ✗ Complete any part of projects for students ✗ Provide answers to student research questions

Academic integrity and authentication responsibilities

Supervisors play a crucial role in ensuring student projects maintain academic integrity throughout the process. Their responsibilities include:

- Monitoring student work throughout the process to confirm authenticity.
- Guiding students on the ethical use of technology including their use of AI.
- Ensuring students understand and follow proper citation practices.
- Guiding students to recognise and avoid plagiarism.
- Ensuring students are familiar with ethical guidelines for the RP.
- Confirming that external assistance (if any) is properly acknowledged.
- Completing final authentication of submissions.

Communication strategies

- Establish regular check-ins and maintain consistency.
- Encourage students to come prepared with specific questions and updates about ethical analyses.
- Foster honest communication about challenges and concerns in research or thinking.
- Model note-taking during meetings and follow-up on action items.
- Maintain professional and respectful communication.
- Create environments where students feel comfortable asking for feedback, advice and information.

Optimising feedback opportunities

- Encourage students to request specific feedback, especially about analyses.
- Practise active listening and provide opportunities for clarifying questions.
- Encourage reflection on feedback before taking action or inaction.
- Support documentation of feedback and responses in learning journals.
- Facilitate additional perspectives through peer feedback sessions.
- Use formal meetings to support milestone reflection activities.

Fostering learner independence

- Support student ownership of project timelines and ethical explorations.
- Encourage independent decision-making while providing support when needed.
- Develop student problem-solving skills rather than providing solutions.
- Where expertise permits, provide examples of reflective practice and ethical reasoning from your own professional experience.
- Gradually reduce support as students build confidence.
- Help students take responsibility for their own work while maintaining pride in finished products.

Best practices for RP supervision

Creating supportive learning environments

- Establish clear expectations for supervisory relationships from the beginning.
- Foster environments of mutual respect and professional collaboration.
- Encourage risk-taking and intellectual curiosity within appropriate boundaries.
- Model reflective practice in your own professional interactions when possible.
- Celebrate student growth and achievement throughout the process.

Managing multiple supervisory relationships

- Develop systems such as keeping a spreadsheet or using project management tools for tracking individual student progress and needs.
- Maintain consistent communication standards across all supervisory relationships.
- Balance individual student needs with available time and resources.
- Coordinate with other supervisors and coordinators to share best practices.
- Document supervisory interactions for accountability and improvement.

Professional development for supervisors

- Stay current with IB assessment criteria and expectations.
- Participate in professional development opportunities related to ethics education when possible.
- Engage with colleagues to discuss challenging supervisory situations.
- Reflect on your own supervisory practice and seek feedback from coordinators.
- Maintain awareness of current research and best practices in project-based learning.

Partnership in ethical thinking growth and professional development

RP supervisors serve as partners in students' RP journey that focus specifically on ethical thinking and decision-making in students' chosen career fields. Supervisors can bring expertise, guidance, and support in helping students understand their chosen ethical dilemmas, while students bring curiosity, initiative, and authentic engagement with complex ethical issues. Together, they create learning experiences that not only meet RP requirements but also contribute to student development as ethical thinkers, critical analysts, and professional future practitioners.

The supervisory relationship is designed to support student growth in their RP journey while ensuring projects remain authentically student's own work. The ethical dilemmas students explore and the perspectives they consider will challenge them to think deeply about professional responsibilities and ethical decision-making. The supervisor's role is to guide this process while allowing students to maintain ownership of their learning and personal position on their ethical dilemma.

This supervisory partnership models the type of mentoring relationships students will encounter throughout their careers, particularly when facing complex ethical decisions. The skills students develop – communication, professionalism, receiving feedback, independent problem-solving, and ethical reasoning – will serve them well in university and beyond as they navigate the ethical challenges of their chosen professions.

A commitment to effective supervision directly impacts student success and contributes to the overall quality of the CP. By understanding and embracing the full scope of supervisory responsibilities, supervisors and coordinators help ensure that each student's RP becomes a meaningful capstone experience that prepares them for ethical leadership in their future careers.

Reflective project moderation and standardisation practice

While the reflective project is an externally assessed component of the Career-related Programme, many schools and coordinators have found that implementing collaborative **standardisation** and **moderation** practices significantly enhances the quality of supervisor feedback and the accuracy of predicated grades.

Standardisation typically occurs after students submit their refined drafts following their presentation of findings. It involves supervisors calibrating their understanding of the assessment criteria to provide consistent, high-quality feedback and aligned guidance for students' draft revisions.

Moderation normally takes place after students submit their final projects and involves supervisors working together to check the fairness and accuracy of the predicated grades. Although not formally required by the IB for externally assessed components, many schools conduct this practice as a voluntary best practice to ensure predicated grades are accurate, consistent, and fair across all students and supervisors.

Both processes can be conducted internally within your school, externally with partner schools, or as a combination of both.

Benefits of collaborative standardisation and moderation practices

These collaborative practices - whether internal, external, or combined - provide several important advantages:

- **For marking consistency and predicated grade accuracy:**
  - Supervisors gain exposure to a wider range of student work and alternative formats, calibrating their understanding of achievement levels.
  - Comparative discussion with peers helps establish benchmarks and align understanding of the assessment criteria.
  - Regular participation in these processes improves feedback given to students, as well as accuracy and consistency of predicted grades over time.
  - Students benefit from more effective, criteria-aligned feedback on their drafts, and more reliable predicted grades that better reflect their final external assessment outcomes.
- **For supervisor professional development:**
  - Hands-on practice in applying criteria to diverse student work is more effective professional development than theoretical training alone.
  - Supervisors, especially those who are new to the process, benefit significantly from seeing examples of student work across different achievement levels, formats and topics.
  - Collaborative discussion with more experienced supervisors provides valuable mentoring and confidence-building for new or less experienced supervisors.
  - Supervisors develop shared language and understanding around their interpretation of criteria.
  - External collaboration also exposes supervisors to diverse approaches and perspectives from other schools and educational contexts.
- **For student support:**
  - When supervisors have a clearer, more consistent understanding of the assessment criteria, they provide more targeted and concrete feedback to students.
  - Timely, criteria-aligned feedback after the draft submission allows students to make meaningful revisions.

- Students benefit from having supervisors who are confident, well-calibrated, and aligned with programme standards.
- Students receive clearer signals about their progress relative to external assessment.

- **For programme quality:**
  - Collaborative practice and networks create ongoing professional learning communities around the RP.
  - More accurate predicted grades support better student preparation and realistic goal-setting.
  - Fairness and consistency checks protect students and enhance programme integrity and outcomes.
  - External partnerships foster a community of practice around RP excellence.

Implementation of standardisation and moderation practices

Both processes can be conducted internally, externally, or a combination of both. There are normally three stages for both practices:

1. **Preparation:**
   - **Shared access point:** Organise a shared digital folder (such as Google Drive, Teams, or other equivalent platforms) where anonymous RP samples are uploaded
   - **Student work sample selection:**
     - *Internal approach*: If you have a large number of supervisors, you can establish small working groups (3-4 supervisors per group). Each supervisor in the group selects one anonymous student RP draft sample and uploads it to a shared group folder.
     - *External approach*: Each participating school can collect three samples representing the range of achievement - one high, one mid-range, and one low - without indicating which is which, and upload them to the shared folder.
   - **Distribute resources:** Share the RP assessment criteria and grade descriptors with all participants.

2. **Pre-standardisation/moderation**
   - Send supervisors a digital marking form (Google form or equivalent) or marking template.
   - Ask each supervisor to independently review and assess selected students' samples using the assessment criteria and grade descriptors, avoiding peer influence during the marking process.
   - Collect preliminary marks as well as feedback or comments from all participants to identify areas of alignment and divergence in scoring.

3. Standardisation/moderation meeting

- Convene a meeting with all participants either in-person or virtually.
- Select a few students' samples where marking discrepancies are greatest for focused discussion and debate.
- Use these as **anchor samples**, or reference points to align understanding of the assessment criteria, grade descriptors, and their application.
- Clarify criteria interpretation and develop shared language for describing achievement levels.
- Discuss implications:
  - *For standardisation practice*: The discussion will focus around the feedback supervisors will provide to students for revision so students receive more consistent, criteria-aligned feedback on their drafts and have clear direction for meaningful revision.
  - *For moderation practice*: The discussion will surround implications for predicated grades and work toward consensus on final agreed markings for the selected samples, checking that grades assigned are appropriate, consistent, fair, and accurate.

Flexibility in standardisation and moderation approaches

Schools have the flexibility to determine how they implement these practices. The choice of approach depends on your school's needs, cohort size, available resources, and access to collaborative partnerships. Smaller working groups can be established if your school has a large number of students and supervisors involved. These groups typically consist of 3-4 supervisors who work together to review and provide feedback on student samples, making the process more manageable while maintaining quality assurance.

Considerations for establishing your standardisation and moderation practices

When establishing or organising your school's standardisation and moderation practices, consider the following:

- **Assess your needs and context:** Determine whether internal standardisation and/or moderation would benefit your supervisor's professional development and your students' overall learning experience and outcome. Consider your cohort size and whether working in smaller groups would be appropriate.
- **Decide on your approach:** Choose whether to implement internal practices, external practices, or a combination of both. Consider your school's capacity and access to partner schools.
- **Start with one phase:** Consider beginning with either standardisation or moderation before implementing both.
- **Find partners** (if pursuing external practices)**:** Identify other CP schools regionally or globally (ideally with similar RP implementation timelines) willing to participate in a pilot of collaborative standardisation and/or moderation.
- **Use technology:** Google drive, Teams, or other equivalent digital platforms for file sharing and data collection make both processes manageable and cost effective, supporting both in-person and virtual collaboration.
- **Schedule strategically:** Plan for standardisation sessions after draft submission and moderation sessions after final project submission.

- **Establish smaller working groups** (if needed)**:** If your school or the collaborative group has many supervisors involved, divide them into smaller working groups (3-4 supervisors per group) to manage the workload while maintaining quality oversight.
- **Communicate with supervisors:** Help supervisors understand the purpose, value, and structure of each process they will participate in.
- **Document and reflect:** Keep records of standardisation and/or moderation discussions to inform supervisor training and programme improvements. They are also useful evidence of collaboration for your school's ongoing programme evaluation.
- **Make it sustainable:** Build the processes into your annual RP calendar as expected continuous professional practice.

The investment in structured standardisation and moderation processes yields significant returns in feedback quality, predicted grade accuracy, supervisor confidence, and ultimately, student success on the reflective project.

Commitment to success

Approach the RP as the pinnacle of each student's CP journey. This 4,000-word exploration into a career-linked authentic ethical dilemma is more than an academic exercise, it is where students hone their ethical decision-making skills that will steer them as principled future professionals. Champion their curiosity, structure the 50 hours of independent inquiry with purposeful milestones and turn every supervisory conference into a coaching moment that transforms into growth. By empowering students to choose their own medium – essay, graphic novel, podcast or film – that best amplifies their voice, you help them weave together every strand of their CP experience and stride forward with resilience, ethical courage, and a mindset to thrive and flourish in their future life and career.

Key takeaways: Chapter 11

- The RP is a culminating experience for students in the CP.
- The knowledge and skills developed throughout the CP experience can connect to and support students in their RP learning journey.
- The RP brings together learning from DP courses, CRS and CP core components.
- This alignment uniquely prepares students for the RP, using experiences, knowledge and skills gained across the CP curriculum.
- The RP empowers students to explore ethical dilemmas related to their personal and professional goals and aspirations.
- The skills practised through the RP – critical inquiry, ethical reasoning and reflection – are valuable for further academic study and employment.
- Completing the RP offers students a tangible example of academic engagement in a relevant field, which can be used in university admissions, whether as a portfolio piece or as a discussion point in interviews.

- Ample opportunities for reflection ensure the learning journey is relevant and applicable to students' future ambitions and endeavours.
- The RP supervisory role encompasses five distinct phases, each with specific focus areas and supervisory responsibilities.
- Balancing RP supervisory support with students' independence is crucial for maintaining authentic student work.
- The formal review of one complete RP draft represents a critical supervisory intervention requiring careful preparation.
- Academic integrity and authentication are ongoing RP supervisory responsibilities throughout the process.
- Effective RP supervision contributes significantly to student development in ethical reasoning and professional skills.
- RP supervisory practice should model the professional mentoring relationships students will encounter in their careers.
- The incorporation of moderation and standardisation practices offers several important benefits for both students and educators.

Key terms

anchor samples: Exemplary student work samples selected during standardisation or moderation meetings that represent different achievement levels and serve as reference points to align understanding of the assessment criteria and calibrate grading.

moderation: A collaborative process conducted after students submit final projects in which supervisors work together to check the fairness, accuracy, and consistency of predicated grades assigned to students.

standardisation: A collaborative process conducted after students submit their drafts in which supervisors calibrate their understanding of the assessment criteria to ensure consistent, high-quality feedback is provided to students for their subsequent revisions.

12 Frequently asked questions

Personal and professional skills

Addressing the learning outcomes

Is there a recommended or required sequence for addressing the learning outcomes?

In short, 'no'. Schools maintain the flexibility to sequence and structure their personal and professional skills (PPS) course in a way that best meets the needs of their students. However, there are a few key aspects to take into consideration when deciding how you will structure and sequence your course.

Meet your students where they are. Get to know the cohort of students entering CP 1 as best as you can before they begin their Career-related Programme (CP) journey. This will inform your decisions in sequencing the course in a way that best supports their needs.

Consider the reflective project (RP) timeline. Some skills development is more urgent than others, depending on what is expected from students at different points in their RP journey. Make sure that the skills development and sequencing of PPS align with the expectations for students from your RP timeline.

Consider the introductory unit in language and cultural studies (LCS) – all the learning from this unit is relevant to PPS. With careful planning, PPS inquiries near the beginning of the course can coincide with the content of LCS to provide a rich and meaningful experience for students to begin both components. This could lead to accelerated skill development across all four PPS skill domains and provide students with opportunities to explore ethics and ethical thinking in multiple contexts.

Consider the introduction and orientation to community engagement (CE). Like the introductory unit in LCS, much of what will be explored in CE will be of relevance to PPS. Collaboratively planning alongside the CE coordinator will allow you to make the best use of all the learning from across the CP core in the early PPS inquiries.

Keeping the course student-centred

How do I ensure the course remains student-centred while meeting the learning outcomes?

Here are a few strategies to support you in doing this.

Plan with your students: Schedule as much planning time with students as possible to ensure your PPS course is student-centred and designed to meet their needs and aspirations. If you are finding it challenging to make time for planning, consider using online surveys or feedback tools with your students.

Schedule time for student-designed inquiries in your PPS course outline: If you want to maintain a focus on specific learning outcomes, restrict the inquiries to those outcomes, but allow students to design how they are explored and developed.

Conduct regular check-ins on student portfolios: Maintain awareness of each student's progress towards the learning outcomes. The knowledge and understanding of your students' development will enable you to pivot if necessary, ensuring that all students meet all learning outcomes.

Maintaining the ethics focus

Applied ethics was a theme in the previous PPS guide, but it is not represented as one of the skill domains in the 2025 guide; does that mean there is less of a focus on ethics now?

No – this is not the case. If anything, ethics has an increased role to play in PPS, and across the broader implementation of the CP core from 2025 onwards. Ethics, ethical thinking, ethical decision-making and exploring one's ethical and moral values are all essential to successful engagement with and completion of all four CP core components. Ethics is integrated throughout PPS – it is included in two of the skill domains (Thinking skills and Intercultural understanding) and is represented clearly in the fifth learning outcome.

Curating a digital portfolio

What applications and platforms are best for curating a digital portfolio?

There are a variety of platforms and applications currently available, and with evolving technology, the possibilities for digital portfolios will undoubtedly continue to change. To make a decision that best suits your students, schools should consider applications and platforms with which they are already familiar and which conform to any local limitations or requirements. Consider the following questions when determining how to approach the creation of digital portfolios.

- Which platform(s) can most effectively support students in creating and maintaining a digital portfolio?
- Do they provide students with an opportunity to use multiple types of media within their portfolio?
- Can teachers provide feedback directly through this application or platform?
- Could it also be used across the other core components to ensure consistency and support students in becoming more comfortable and confident in using it?
- If not, can your school invest in researching which application or platform would best suit your context, and then purchase and train staff and students in that tool?
- Alternatively, would you consider allowing students to choose the application or platform that they feel most comfortable using for their digital portfolio?

Reviewing/assessing student progress

How often should I review or assess student progress?

Assessing student progress frequently allows you to adapt inquiries and the overall course outline to best suit your students' growth. Formative assessment should occur regularly throughout an inquiry to keep you apprised of your students' knowledge, understanding and progress at that moment, allowing you to be agile with your teaching. This will help you guide your students through the remainder of the inquiry, and formative assessment may occur as frequently as every lesson through small check-ins. More robust, summative assessments may take place less often, perhaps once or twice throughout an inquiry, but give a better understanding of how your students have applied their learning. This feedback can support you and your students in deciding upon the next steps in their PPS learning journey.

Supporting struggling students

What should I do if a student struggles to meet one or more learning outcomes?

This could be addressed in several ways. For example:

Student enquiry: Create an inquiry with the student, allowing them to engage with the learning outcome(s) in question using the most relevant approach for them. Making the inquiry as specific as possible to their context may help them engage with the content and the learning outcome(s).

Alternative assessment: Consider a different style of assessment that focuses on an inquiry or inquiries that have already been covered. Perhaps the student was able to learn and make progress towards the learning outcome(s) but was unable to demonstrate this through the assessment modes in use. By designing a different method of assessment, students can re-engage with the learning outcome(s) and highlight their growth and progress in different ways, honouring their prior learning.

Extended timeline: If necessary, use the entire time available for the PPS course. Most schools will complete this course before the IB exams begin; however, it is acceptable for it to continue throughout the exam period if a student needs additional time to complete their portfolio and ensure progress has been made towards all learning outcomes. However, note that this could put students under additional pressure during the exam period, so it should only be considered if essential, and should always be managed carefully.

Collaborating with other teachers

What level of collaboration is expected between PPS teachers and other CP core component coordinators/teachers/mentors/supervisors?

The core is designed to be integrated, with each component complementing the others. Consequently, the better the collaboration among all staff members responsible for delivering the CP core, the smoother its implementation will be. The more designated planning time can be given to CP core staff, the more cohesive the delivery can be. This can only benefit the student and staff experience if the collaboration is well supported and guided by the CP coordinator.

Personalising the PPS course

How can I personalise the PPS course to match students' career-related pathways?

If you work in a school that only offers one career-related study (CRS), design your PPS course with that in mind. You can get highly specific in your inquiries to focus on the professional elements of that career field and the personal considerations that professionals in that area may need to be more conscious of. If your school offers multiple CRS pathways and your PPS classes will consist of students studying in very different pathways, then focus more on how you frame your questioning within lessons so that each student can extract their learning in their unique career-related context. Utilise support from CRS teachers and providers to help you do this, as they can assist you in integrating CRS expertise into each of your PPS inquiries that require it.

Helping students to take ownership

What strategies help students take ownership of their learning journey?

Explaining the purpose of PPS and the wider CP is of paramount importance when cultivating student engagement and ownership of learning. CP students should be entering the programme specialising in an area of passion and/or expertise for them. PPS, the other CP core components, the CRS, and their Diploma

Programme (DP) subject choices should all be aligned with their aspirations, needs, and wants. Making it clear to students that they already have so much influence on what and how they learn will support them in seeing the value of their personalised CP experience and what it can offer them. Involving them in the design process of inquiries and encouraging their position as stakeholders will also reinforce the students' sense of agency. This is their journey, and the more they put into it, the more impactful it will be on their personal and professional skill development.

Reflective project

Keeping the course student-centred

Who is responsible for teaching ethics to RP students?

Ethics is a common topic across all four CP core components, so there should be ample opportunities for students to engage with ethical thinking and ethical decision-making throughout their CP experience. It is advisable for the CP core teaching team to plan and determine how student learning engagements can connect and spiral across the curriculum to ensure students have sufficient opportunity to acquire, develop and apply their knowledge prior to the final production of their RP. The PPS course can support students in this endeavour as various aspects of ethics can be woven across multiple inquiries.

An example of spiralling ethics within the CP Core might be:

- students are introduced early on to an ethical dilemma relevant to their community during the guided learning portion of their CE component and are asked to identify how they might approach it and to justify their thinking
- simultaneously, in PPS, students can be introduced to a variety of ethical principles or philosophies, with examples of each
- students could be tasked with identifying ethical dilemmas straight from the news or within their CRS and learn to recognise the different ethical principles involved
- explorations, debates and discussions in any of the core components can help students first define their own personal values, then practise making theoretical decisions followed by the application of their thinking to real-world scenarios.

Schools might also provide direct instruction on ethics to an entire student cohort. This instruction might take place in PPS, as suggested in the inquiry examples in this book. Or it could be initiated with a full cohort workshop followed with more specific reinforcement and teaching throughout the CP core and in the CRS classes. Schools may teach ethics as a standalone topic or integrate ethical concepts throughout the different components, DP or CRS curricula. Whatever method or types of activities chosen, schools must ensure that students can develop, apply and refine the ethical thinking skills necessary for success in the RP.

Creating different formats

How will students know how to create the different formats allowed for their RP?

This is another area where the PPS, other core components and DP subjects can help students prepare for the RP. Exposure is critical – whether in the types of texts and materials used for instruction and exploration or the types of texts and products created during learning engagements, the more students interact with different formats and modalities, the more familiar they will become with them. Students might also be connected to different teachers or other community stakeholders who can support them in understanding the requirements and conventions of different formats. For example, students who are interested in film or podcasts but who are not taking a film or media class might get involved in a media club or other school-related opportunity. They might also begin a personal inquiry into local outlets (such as community clubs or classes) to develop their skills.

Helping students as a non-expert

Do the RP coordinators and RP supervisors need to be experts in the students' career fields to support them through the RP journey?

Often, supervisors or coordinators will not be experts in all fields that students wish to pursue. A familiarity with the CRS options offered at the school is sufficient for supervisors or coordinators to support students through their RP journey, as their main role is really to monitor, motivate and provide feedback. It is far more important that RP supervisors and coordinators have a good understanding of the RP requirements, and a general knowledge of appropriate research processes than of students' career fields.

Determining the presentation process

Does the RP presentation have to take place in the PPS class?

The method and format of the students' RP presentation is not outlined by the IB, so it is up to schools to determine the process for students' RP presentations. The presentations can be done in any way that fits the school context – for example, in a classroom setting, as a school-wide or community exhibition, online streaming with an audience, or after school in small groups who have the same supervisor.

Appendix

Reflective project proposal form

Use the information and example here to help your student plan their reflective project proposal and ensure it is effective, thoughtful and complete.

The purpose of the reflective project proposal is to clarify your research plan, articulate your objectives and lay the groundwork for successful project development. It serves as both an initial roadmap and a tool for repeated refinement throughout your RP journey. While the IB does not require you to have a project proposal, completing one before embarking on independent research will help you set clear expectations and guide your learning journey every step of the way.

Key components of the reflective project proposal

Title, objectives and rationale:

- Title in the form of a research question – a specific question for inquiry
- Objectives – the ethical dilemma, investigation aims and intended skills or knowledge to develop. For example:
  - Explore best practices for inclusive casting without sacrificing artistic integrity
  - Investigate historical context and audience impact
  - Examine stakeholder perceptions and formulate practical recommendations
- Rationale – link the topic to your career-related interests, personal motivations and the broader relevance to your professional field.

Resources, research and methodology:

- Resources: List books, articles, interviews, databases, online forums, and other resources. Distinguish between primary (interviews, surveys etc.) and secondary (published articles, reports etc.) sources.
- Research: Identify the areas to be covered (historical context, industry practices, cultural perspectives, etc.). Consider impact on community, stakeholders, and ethical dimensions.
- Methodology: Describe how you'll gather information and ensure validity. Include strategies to minimise bias and limitations. Commit to diverse data sources and transparency
- Activities and timescale: Include a timeline with estimated completion dates for each phase and specific milestones

How to use this example proposal:

- Use the sample headings and structure to frame your own proposal.
- Refer to the timescale for pacing your own RP learning journey.
- Adopt referenced documentation strategies (such as using OPVL analysis and correct citation formats) shown in the example.
- Reference any school-supplied templates for additional guidance.

Best practices for proposal preparation:

- Be clear and specific: Each section should be focused and show your personal engagement.
- Connect to your career interests: Root your project rationale closely to your interested career field and professional aspiration.
- Plan for iteration: Use supervisor feedback to improve your proposal and project as you work.
- Anticipate challenges: Identify potential obstacles and include contingency plans in your timescale.
- Document resources and references: Track your sources carefully and use recognised academic formats (APA, MLA, etc.)
- Reflective integration: Let your proposal stages link to reflective journal entries throughout your RP development.

Your school may use a different format to guide the project proposal, or you may adapt the example and formats to fit your own needs. The important thing is to include all required sections and update your proposal as your thinking evolves during the reflective project.

Summary checklist

- ❑ Title or research question
- ❑ Objectives and rationale
- ❑ Detailed list of resources
- ❑ Research plan and areas
- ❑ Methodology and bias mitigation strategy
- ❑ Activities and timescale
- ❑ Supervisor feedback
- ❑ Plans for documentation and referencing

Example

PART A: Student proposal (to be completed by the student)
Section 1: Title, objectives and rationale
Title or working title of the reflective project (in the form of a research question):
Objectives (What is the ethical dilemma of your reflective project? What do you want to find out? What do you hope to achieve by the end of the project? What are some of the knowledge and skills you want to utilise or develop further through this process?)
Rationale (How is it relevant to your career-related field or subject of study? What are your motivations in undertaking research in this area? Why is this topic important to you?):

Section 2: Resources, research and methodology
Resources (What resources will you need for your research, production of your final product/output, and final presentation/viva voce? e.g library, books, journals, online database, videos, forums and other additional equipment. How do you keep track of your sources and organise them? What systems of academic referencing are you going to use?) *To effectively conduct this project, produce a final output, and prepare for a presentation, I will be using the following sources:* *Primary sources:* • *Secondary sources:* •
Research (What areas of research will you cover? e.g. elders, other ethical dimensions and cultural perspectives) *Context of the issue:* • *Impact on community members/stakeholders:* • *Ethical Dimensions:* • *Cultural perspectives:* • *Practical solutions and best practices:* • *Casting choices:* •
Methodology (How do you plan to collect evidence to help you research perspectives? What are the potential biases and limitations of your research methods? How do you ensure the best research collection for your project?) *Methodology for collecting evidence and researching perspectives:* • *Potential biases and limitations:* • *Ensuring best research collection:* •

Section 3: Activities and timescales	
Activities to be carried out during the project process following the RP journey	**Estimated completion time**
Organise first meeting with supervisor	
Identify possible interviewees	
Create Google forms for theatre community	
Create interview/form questions	
Conduct interviews	
Organise second meeting with supervisor	
Conduct research on secondary sources	
Analyse and organise responses (form and interview)	
Organise third meeting with supervisor	
First draft	
Organise fourth meeting with supervisor	
Second draft	
Organise fifth meeting with supervisor	
Oral presentation of RP	
FINAL	

Viva voce sentence starters

Use the following sentences to clarify the ideas you might discuss in your viva voce.

Process-related

I chose this topic/ethical dilemma because ...

Initially, I hoped to discover ...

The key findings from my research were ...

They helped me gain a deeper understanding of the ethical dilemma by ...

The conclusions I have drawn about my ethical dilemma are ...

Having completed my project, the additional discoveries I have made are ...

Reflecting on my research process, the main challenges I encountered were ...

The methodology I used for my research was ...

I decided to approach it this way because ...

The limitations of my research approach were ...

Some additional questions I have about the issue that could lead to further investigation are ...

The challenges I encountered were ...

I overcame them by ...

The unexpected or contradictory findings during my research were ...

I navigated and worked through them by ...

The things I would have done differently in my research process were ...

Because ...

During my research, what I discovered about the complexity of ethical decision-making is ...

Throughout the research process, my understanding of the ethical dilemma evolved from ...

to ...

Project-related

The ethical frameworks or theories I utilised to analyse the ethical dilemma were ...

They helped to inform my understanding and conclusions by ...

If I were to conduct further research, the specific areas or aspects I would explore would be ...

This is because ...

The most significant insights I gained from my reflective project were ...

They changed my perspective on ...

Engaging with the reflective project deepened my understanding of the ethical complexities within my chosen career field by ...

Personal growth-related

Engaging with this ethical dilemma influenced my way of thinking about related issues or topics by ...

This is because ...

Insights I gained about the dilemma include ...

Insights about my career field include ...

Insights I had about myself are ...

The most valuable skills or knowledge that I have developed throughout my reflective project learning journey are ...

I envision applying them in my future career or education by ...

Reflecting on my personal growth, the things I have learned about myself through engaging with the reflective project are ...

Impact-related

Looking back at my reflective project learning journey, the most rewarding aspect for me was ...

The most challenging aspect of my learning journey was ...

I overcame it by ...

I think this experience of completing the reflective project will impact my future work / studies in terms of ethical decision making by ...

The advice I would give to future students undertaking the reflective project or embarking on a similar research process are ...

My reflective project contributes to my understanding of professional ethics by demonstrating ...

And by highlighting the importance of ...

PPS Inquiry 5: Cultural identity in a globalised workplace

Inquiry overview:	This inquiry encourages students to explore how cultural identity influences communication, relationships and professional interactions. As global workplaces become more interconnected, understanding and navigating cultural differences is an essential skill. Through interviews, case studies, simulations and reflective activities, students will investigate the impact of their own identity and develop the intercultural understanding necessary to thrive in diverse environments.		
Concepts:	Identities Connections Perspectives	**Contexts:**	Language and cultural studies Professional life Community engagement
Content:	Surface vs. deep culture (iceberg model) Factors shaping cultural identity Intercultural communication and miscommunication Empathy, respect, and active listening Strategies for navigating cultural challenges in professional settings	**Skills:**	**Interpersonal** Collaboration and networking Communication **Intercultural understanding** Empathy Social awareness
Learner Profile Attributes:	Open-minded Communicator Reflective Caring		
Learning outcomes:	**LO2:** Develop and apply communication and interpersonal skills in various contexts **LO4:** Develop and apply intercultural understanding in a variety of contexts		
Length of inquiry:	Year 2 15 hours (minimum)	**Connections across the programme:**	**Reflective project:** Prepares students to examine perspectives in ethical dilemmas. **Language and cultural studies:** Reinforces appreciation of diverse linguistic and cultural backgrounds.

PPS Inquiry 5: Cultural identity in a globalised workplace

Stage	Learning engagements	Time	Output
Focus question	How do cultural backgrounds influence professional identity and shape interactions in a globalised workplace?		
Focus	**Task:** Learning engagement A: The cultural iceberg and identity mapping **Purpose**: To help students reflect on their own cultural identity and develop awareness of the visible and invisible aspects of culture that shape who we are. **Preparation:** Prepare visuals or slides explaining the 'cultural iceberg' model. Provide an identity mapping template (e.g. the iceberg model) or allow for creative/free-form expression. Prepare sample sentence starters (e.g. 'One part of my identity people can see is...', 'One part they usually can't is...'). **Instructions:** Begin with a short video or image comparing surface and deep culture. Emphasise that culture is more than nationality – include family structure, religion, gender roles, humour, time orientation. Introduce the 'cultural Iceberg' model using the visuals or slides you have prepared. Ask students to complete their own 'cultural identity map', labelling influences such as language, values, traditions, habits and communication styles. Put students in small groups and ask them to compare icebergs, using the following questions: – What is visible to others? – What is often misunderstood? – How might this affect communication in a team? Encourage students to be respectful when sharing and allow them to keep private any parts of their identity they do not wish to discuss. **Optional extension:** Students could write a short paragraph in response to the question: 'What part of your identity is misunderstood the most, and why might that be?'	2 hours	Cultural identity iceberg graphic Discussion notes

<table>
<tr>
<td>Explore</td>
<td>Task: Learning engagement B: Workplace culture case studies

Purpose: To explore real-life examples of cultural misunderstanding and successful intercultural collaboration in professional environments.

Note: The Culture Map by Erin Myer is very useful in exploring this topic. If possible, add a book study to this inquiry, or use some examples from the book in your case studies, as well as the solutions and suggestions there.

Preparation:

Select or create three or four short workplace case studies involving cultural clashes or diversity successes (e.g. team communication, hierarchy, time management).

Instructions:

Organise students into rotating discussion groups or stations. They should rotate through the workplace case studies you have prepared, analysing each one using a shared template, identifying the key issues and the cultural dimensions involved. They should also propose inclusive solutions.

Students work in groups to analyse using guiding questions:
– What cultural perspectives are involved?
– What worked or did not work?
– What assumptions were made?

As students rotate, they should add to the shared template. This could have the guiding questions on it. By the end, the class will have a group summary for each scenario. This template can be paper for adding notes, an online PPT slide, or any other creative solution.

When all groups have reviewed all the case studies, they should take it in turns to present one case to the class.

Afterwards, have a whole class debriefing discussion on communication styles (direct vs. indirect, individualism vs. collectivism).

Optional extension: Students could connect one case study to their own CRS or future workplace, discussing how cultural awareness would help them succeed in that field.</td>
<td>2.5 hours</td>
<td>Group summary chart

Class presentation</td>
</tr>
</table>

	Task: Learning engagement C: Empathy interview **Purpose:** To build intercultural understanding through listening to and learning from someone with a different cultural background or workplace experience. **Preparation:** Create an interview template that includes prompts such as: – What is one way your culture influences how you work or communicate?' – 'Have you ever felt misunderstood in a work or school setting?' **Instructions:** Review interview etiquette and empathy-focused listening strategies with students. Hand out the interview template you have created. Allow time in class for students to plan and rehearse the questions they are going to ask. Frame the task as building understanding, not judging others' choices Ask students to interview someone from a different cultural background (classmate, teacher, parent or community member) about the following issues: – Professional or school experiences working in diverse teams – Challenges or misunderstandings encountered – Strategies that supported inclusion. Afterwards, students should write a reflection focusing on what surprised or challenged their assumptions. If students need more support with this, offer sentence frames, such as 'I used to think ... now I realise ....' **Optional extension:** Students should turn their reflections into a short written profile or podcast-style recording to share in class.	2 hours	Interview write-up One-page personal reflection
Act	**Task:** Learning engagement D: Cultural simulation challenge **Purpose:** To allow students to experience intercultural miscommunication and problem-solving in action by working through a collaborative group simulation with conflicting cultural norms.	2 hours	Group event plan Team reflection

<table>
<tr>
<td></td>
<td>
Preparation:
Create role cards for 4–6 different cultural identities with distinct communication styles, time values or group preferences.
Design a shared group task (e.g. planning a product launch where team members from different cultural backgrounds have conflicting approaches to decision-making, communication, and time management).
Prepare debrief discussion questions, such as:
– What challenges did you face when trying to collaborate with team members who had different cultural values and communication styles?
– How did your own cultural assumptions influence the way you approached the task and interacted with others?
– What strategies helped resolve conflicts or misunderstandings, and how would you approach a similar situation in the future?
Instructions:
Divide students into groups, and provide each group with a set of role cards, each representing a different cultural identity with distinct communication styles, values, and preferences.
Instruct students to collaborate on the task, role-playing the cultural identity assigned to them. They must work together to solve the problem, but the challenges they face will stem from the differing values and norms of their assigned cultural roles.
Clearly explain to students that they must fully embrace and act according to the cultural norms, communication styles, and values outlined in their role cards during the task.
Afterwards, come together as a class to discuss the following questions:
– 'What made the collaboration difficult? What challenged you?'
– 'How did your assumptions influence your choices?'
– 'What would you do differently next time?'
Optional extension: Students could create a visual or written reflection describing what this simulation taught them about working with people different from myself.'
</td>
<td></td>
<td></td>
</tr>
</table>

	Task: Learning engagement E: Diversity and inclusion pitch **Purpose**: To apply intercultural understanding by creating a persuasive message that promotes inclusion in professional or academic environments. **Preparation:** Provide a checklist or success criteria for effective communication to be used in the peer feedback session. **Instructions:** Explain to students that they are going to create a pitch or poster campaign encouraging a school, business or CRS-related organisation to value cultural inclusion. The presentation should be grounded in at least one real story or insight from the inquiry (e.g. interview, simulation, case study). Offer sample success stories or DEI workplace campaigns as examples. Provide format options for students to choose from: mini-presentation, digital poster, one-page proposal, short video. Students then write their pitch (1–2 minutes long) or poster campaign, encouraging employers to build diverse, inclusive teams. Remind them to focus on real examples from interviews/case studies. Organise a peer feedback session before students make final revisions to their pitch – use the success criteria created in the preparation. **Optional extension:** Students could send their pitch to a real school leader or CRS partner and invite feedback or dialogue.	2 hours	Pitch video/poster Peer feedback notes
Reflect	**Task:** Learning engagement F: Identity and empathy journal **Purpose:** To give students time to process their learning, explore how their cultural understanding has changed, and consider how this may shape future relationships and work habits. **Preparation:** Prepare a set of open-ended reflection prompts, such as: – What did I learn about myself through this inquiry? – What surprised or challenged me the most? – How can empathy help me succeed in a globalised workplace?	2 hours	Portfolio reflection entry

	- What part of your identity do you value more after this inquiry? - What skill (e.g. empathy, flexibility) did you strengthen? - How would you handle a future misunderstanding differently? - Which LO (LO2 or LO4) do you feel most connected to and why? Provide journal format options e.g. notebook, online, or using your school's LMS **Instructions:** Explain to students that they are going to create an 'Identity and empathy journal' to explore how their cultural understanding has changed and assess future impacts. Allow students to choose the format option they would like to create (written journal, audio, video or visual metaphor). Encourage honesty and vulnerability. Consider modelling reflection by sharing your own takeaway. Students then work independently complete a guided reflection using the prompt sheet you have prepared, connecting their personal identity, learning experiences and growth in intercultural understanding. They must identify at least one learning outcome and two skills they developed. **Optional extension:** Students could select one excerpt from their reflection to include in their PPS portfolio with a title and short explanation of why it represents a key moment of growth.		
Share	**Task:** Learning engagement G: Cultural inclusion awareness showcase **Purpose:** To consolidate and communicate learning by creating a product that promotes cultural awareness, empathy and inclusion in a professional or academic environment. **Preparation**: Create a simple checklist or list of success criteria, including: - Clear message or insight - Reference to a learning experience (e.g. interview, simulation, identity map) - Relevance to global workplace or CRS context. Invite the audience in advance: peers, CRS teachers or advisory groups.	2 hours	One creative product that communicates their learning about cultural identity, empathy, and communication in professional life

	Instructions: Explain to students that they are going to create a product that promotes cultural awareness. This can be done individually or in small groups. Allow them to decide what format they would like this product to take (but encourage them to choose a format that challenges them): – a workplace inclusion poster or infographic – a personal reflection speech – a short article or blog post – a group-led roundtable discussion or presentation. Ask students to share their learning about cultural identity and inclusion by designing a creative product that promotes intercultural understanding in a professional context. Give students the checklist you have prepared to refer to when completing their product. Students should highlight a key insight gained from their empathy interview, simulation activity or personal reflection, and explain how this connects to their future goals or CRS. **Optional extension:** Students could submit their product to a school newsletter, website, or community platform. Alternatively, they could lead a short advisory session or workshop to educate others about cultural inclusion.		
Portfolio artifact example	**Selected artefact:** Interview write-up and identity journal **Student reflection:** 'My interview made me realise that even subtle differences, like how people give feedback, can cause tension. I used to think I was open-minded, but now I know that I need to ask more questions before I assume someone's intentions. I feel I've really developed LO4, because I can now explain how cultural perspectives shape our actions.'		

Glossary

anchor samples: exemplary student work samples selected during standardisation or moderation meetings that represent different achievement levels and serve as reference points to align understanding of the assessment criteria and calibrate grading

annotation: a brief explanation that connects an artefact to the concepts, contexts, content, skills and learning outcomes

applied ethics: the branch of ethics that focuses on how ethical theories and principles can be used to address real-world moral questions

artefact: a curated piece of evidence that can be used to demonstrate progress against one or more of the PPS learning outcomes

classroom-level decision-making: decisions about how students are grouped for specific classroom tasks or collaborative projects

course-level decision-making: decisions about how students and teachers are allocated to personal and professional skills classes

CP core teaching team: the staff responsible for delivering the four CP core components: personal and professional skills (PPS), the reflective project (RP), language and cultural studies (LCS) and community engagement (CE)

creativity, activity, service (CAS): a component of the DP core where students engage in experiences that foster personal and interpersonal development

critical thinking: the process of examining a subject or idea carefully and critically, without allowing yourself to be influenced by opinions or feelings

culminating experience: a final academic requirement that demonstrates a student's mastery of the skills and knowledge they have acquired throughout the course

curriculum map: a structured plan showing how the personal and professional skills court will meet all IB requirements

ethical decision-making: the process of choosing a course of action when faced with moral questions or dilemmas; this involves evaluating different options based on your ethical values and considering the consequences for all people affected, to arrive at a responsible and justifiable choice

ethical dilemma: an ethical issue in which someone must choose between conflicting values or actions, each with its own drawbacks; while all ethical dilemmas are ethical issues, not all ethical issues necessarily present a dilemma

ethical thinking: the process of carefully considering right and wrong, and using your values to guide your decisions; this involves critically examining your own beliefs and the possible effects of choices on others to act responsibly and fairly

ethics: moral beliefs, rules and principles about right and wrong

extended essay (EE): a component of the DP core that requires students to embark on an independent, self-directed piece of academic research, developing skills in academic writing, time management and critical thinking

external experts and **industry leads:** professionals from outside the school who can offer specialised knowledge and/or real-world experience relevant to personal and professional skills

formative assessment: ongoing evaluation during inquiries that guides student learning and development

framework: a conceptual structure that organises thinking and provides contexts for understanding relationships between ideas

grading scale: a system used to report level of learner performance, often aligned with other components/ subjects

Higher Level (HL): a level in the Diploma Programme course, comprising a minimum of 240 timetabled hours

high-trust classroom culture: a learning environment where students and teachers feel safe, respected, and open to sharing, learning and challenging ideas together

holistic: of or relating to a belief that different parts of something are interconnected and can only be explained by referring to the whole

IB Communities: moderated forums on MyIB for IB educators to connect, ask questions and share resources

intercultural understanding: the ability to recognise and respect cultural differences and interact effectively with people from different cultural backgrounds

interpersonal skills: the behaviours people use to interact successfully with other people, such as communication, collaboration and teamwork

intrapersonal skills: the strategies people use to understand their own behaviour and emotions, to become more self-aware

Job-a-Like (JAL): a professional gathering of educators with similar roles, used to share best practices and collaborate

leading questions: questions that are phrased in a way that suggests or encourages a particular answer

live-time reporting: the practice of giving parents real-time notifications and feedback about assessments, etc., instead of delivering the information at particular fixed intervals

mentoring: the process of helping or giving advice to a younger or less experienced colleague

micro-credential: a certification that acknowledges the acquisition of specific knowledge, skills and competencies, usually achieved after a short course or programme

moderation: a collaborative process conducted after students submit final projects in which supervisors work together to check the fairness, accuracy, and consistency of predicated grades assigned to students

moderation process: a school-based system for reviewing and aligning feedback, grades and the consistency of the student experience

portfolio: a curated collection of student work showing growth, reflection and achievement across all personal and professional skills outcomes

probing questions: questions that are phrased in an open-ended way to encourage a detailed, informative and perhaps subjective answer

qualitative grade descriptors: detailed written statements that define the characteristics of student performance at each grade level (A–E) for assessment purposes; these are used by supervisors or coordinators to evaluate student work against standardised benchmarks and generate predicted grades based on the quality and depth of demonstrated skills rather than numerical scores

reflexive: able to examine your own thoughts, feelings, beliefs, attitudes and behaviours; in the context of the reflective project, it means being aware of your own assumptions and biases, and understanding how these influence your responses and decisions

source curation: the selection, gathering and presentation of the most useful and relevant sources and information for a particular topic

spiralling progression: a scaffolded approach where students revisit skills and/or concepts across components at increasing levels of complexity

staffing models: sample structures showing how schools of varying size and complexity assign roles based on available personnel and resources

stakeholder: a person, group or community that is affected by or has an interest in something; in the reflective project, this means everyone who might be impacted, whether they are in your own community or in other parts of the world

standardisation: a collaborative process conducted after students submit their drafts in which supervisors calibrate their understanding of the assessment criteria to ensure consistent, high-quality feedback is provided to students for their subsequent revisions

Standard Level (SL): a level in the Diploma Programme course, comprising a minimum of 150 timetabled hours

student-led inquiry: an inquiry planned and directed by the student, encouraging autonomy and personal relevance

summative assessment: formal evaluation at the end of an inquiry to measure achievement of learning outcomes

theory of knowledge (TOK): a component of the DP core that encourages students to explore how knowledge is constructed and understood

timetabling: the process of allocating hours and scheduling staff with a strategic vision to create the optimal conditions for teaching and learning

transversal skills: skills that can be used in a wide variety of situations and settings, rather than being specific to a job or academic discipline

trolley problem: a philosophical ethical dilemma where participants must choose between allowing a runaway trolley to run its course, injuring five people, or actively changing its path so that it only injures one person instead. This is used to introduce ethical thinking and stimulate discussion on bias, values and ethical decision-making.

unintentional overlap: the repetition of similar content or skills across core components without deliberate coordination, potentially reducing efficiency or impact